CARLO
CARRETTO

MODERN SPIRITUAL MASTERS
Robert Ellsberg, Series Editor

Already published:

MODERN SPIRITUAL MASTERS SERIES

CARLO CARRETTO

Selected Writings

Selected with an Introduction by

ROBERT ELLSBERG

ORBIS BOOKS

Maryknoll, New York 10545

Founded in 1970, Orbis Books endeavors to publish works that enlighten the mind, nourish the spirit, and challenge the conscience. The publishing arm of the Maryknoll Fathers and Brothers, Orbis seeks to explore the global dimensions of the Christian faith and mission, to invite dialogue with diverse cultures and religious traditions, and to serve the cause of reconciliation and peace. The books published reflect the views of their authors and do not represent the official position of the Maryknoll Society. To learn more about Maryknoll and Orbis Books, please visit our website at www.maryknoll.org.

Library of Congress Cataloging-in-Publication Data

Carretto, Carlo.
    [Selections. English. 2007]
    Essential writings / Carlo Carretto ; selected with an introduction by
Robert Ellsberg. – Abridged version.
       p. cm. – (Modern spiritual masters)
    Rev. ed. of: Selected writings. 1994.
    Includes bibliographical references (p.   ).
    ISBN-13: 978-1-57075-725-9
    1. Carretto, Carlo. 2. Little Brothers of Jesus – Italy – Biography.
3. Spiritual life – Catholic Church – Doctrines. 4. Monastic and religious
life. I. Ellsberg, Robert, 1955- II. Title.
BX4705.C3183A3 2007
271'.79 – dc22
                                 2007018649

Contents

Introduction

Robert Ellsberg

In December 1954, at the age of forty-four, Carlo Carretto arrived at El Abiodh, a remote oasis in the Saharan desert of Algeria, to enter the novitiate of the Little Brothers of Jesus. For twenty years Carretto had served as a charismatic leader of the Italian youth movement of Catholic Action. At the peak of such an active and public career, Carretto's flight to the desert seemed a curious and puzzling move to many of his friends. In explanation Carretto himself could only say that he felt summoned by a call from God: "Leave everything and come with me into the desert. It is not your acts and deeds that I want: I want your prayer, your love."

Responding to this call, Carretto joined the Little Brothers and spent the next ten years as a desert hermit. As it turned out, however, the flight to solitude hardly led to obscurity. Twenty years later the publication of *Letters from the Desert,* a modern spiritual classic, established Carretto's reputation as one of the most popular religious voices in the world today.

Although he went on to write a dozen books, it was *Letters from the Desert,* based directly on his experience in the desert, that most clearly summarized his message. Among other things, his first book helped to popularize the spirituality of Charles de Foucauld, the modern-day Desert Father whose life and writings inspired the foundation of the Little Brothers, and whose spirit animated all of Carretto's subsequent writings. So much does the influence of Foucauld suffuse these writings that it is important, at the risk of digression, to recall some of the essential features of his life and work.

Charles de Foucauld was born into an aristocratic family in Strasbourg in 1858. An indifferent student, and evidently possessed of a weak character, he trained for a career in the army but was dismissed in 1881 as a result of his scandalous behavior. The enduring benefit of his military service was a fascination with the North African desert, to which he returned under the aegis of the French Geographical Society to undertake a dangerous exploration of Morocco. It was there that the experience of Muslim piety helped prompt in Charles a dramatic recovery of his Catholic faith, changing his character and his life forever. "As soon as I believed that there was a God," he later wrote, "I understood that I could not do anything other than live for him. My religious vocation dates from the same moment as my faith."

A pilgrimage through the Holy Land, following the footsteps of Jesus in the actual towns and countryside where he had walked, made a profound impact. Afterward Foucauld entered the Trappists and spent a number of years in a monastery in Syria. But conventional, monastic life did not satisfy him. If there is an essential insight that impressed Foucauld it was the fact that Jesus, the Son of God, had been a poor man and a worker. As a carpenter in Nazareth Jesus had, in these lowly circumstances, embodied the gospel message in its entirety, before ever announcing it in words.

Having achieved this insight, Foucauld set about trying to put it into practice — at first rather literally. For three years he worked as a servant at a convent of Poor Clares in Nazareth itself. But eventually he realized that "Nazareth" might be anyplace. And so, after seeking ordination, he returned to Algeria, to the oasis of Béni-Abbès on the border of Morocco. His goal was to develop a new model of contemplative religious life, a community of Little Brothers, who would live among the poor in a spirit of service and solidarity. In the constitutions he devised for his planned order, Foucauld wrote, "The whole of our existence, the whole of our lives should cry the Gospel from the rooftops...not by our words but by our lives."

Foucauld spent fifteen years in the desert. When he found the remote Béni-Abbès becoming too congested, he sought greater solitude in Tamanrasset, an area where slavery was still practiced. It was there in 1916 that he met his death, killed by Tuareg rebels. Foucauld had spent many years conceiving and preparing the way for followers who never arrived, and he might well have died with little sense of accomplishment had his spirituality not trained him to look beyond outward appearances. In his famous Prayer of Abandonment he had written: "Father, I abandon myself in Your hands, do with me what You will. For whatever You may do, I thank You. I am ready for all, I accept all, let only Your will be done in me, as in all Your creatures...."

Ultimately, however, the reverberations from Foucauld's solitary witness achieved considerable effect. In 1933, many years after his death, Father René Voillaume and four companions left France for the Sahara. They became the core of the Little Brothers of Jesus. Several years later they were joined by the Little Sisters of Jesus. Both fraternities gradually spread throughout the world, their small communities taking up life among the poor and outcast, first in the Sahara desert, but eventually in many obscure corners of the globe.

It was to such a path in midlife that Carlo Carretto was drawn. According to his friend Arturo Paoli, who had known him in Catholic Action and who preceded him into the desert, "I believe that Carlo Carretto...had a very similar experience to Brother Charles: that same sense of uselessness, that waiting for new opportunities, the hope and frustration, that feeling of emptiness, which are often the signs announcing a manifestation of the Spirit." But for those unaware of his inner struggles, the points of comparison between Carlo, the leader and activist, and Brother Charles, the desert hermit, would have seemed at best remote.

Carretto was born in 1910 in Alessandria, in the northern Piedmont region of Italy. His family, poor country folk, soon moved to Turin, where he was raised in an atmosphere of traditional piety. Carlo was the third of six children, four of whom were to enter religious life; one of his younger brothers became a bishop in Thailand. Carlo was educated at the Salesian Oratory and at eighteen became a primary school teacher. He went on to take a degree in history and philosophy and became a school headmaster in Sardinia. However, as a result of clashes with the fascist regime, he was relieved of his post and actually held under guard before being sent back to Piedmont. There, as a result of continuing political difficulties, he was struck from the register of headmasters and placed under surveillance.

But by this time Carretto's energies had found a new outlet in the dynamic youth movement of Catholic Action. This movement, which was particularly strong in Italy and the Catholic countries of Europe and Latin America, represented an exciting effort to mobilize lay people in advancing the religious and social message of the Church. Though directed by the hierarchy, the emphasis of Catholic Action was on the active role of the laity, especially students and young people, in bringing the gospel message to bear on the moral and social issues of the day.

Carretto always spoke affectionately about the impact of the movement on his life: "It took me by the hand and walked with me, it fed me with the Word, it offered me friendship, it taught me how to fight, it helped me know Christ, it inserted me alive into a living reality." Soon his life was absorbed in meetings, conferences, and a blur of organizing. He quickly rose to a position of leadership in the movement, which he clearly regarded as a form of religious vocation — so much so that he felt a personal call to celibacy. In 1945 he was invited to Rome by Pope Pius XII to set up the Association of Catholic Teachers, and the next year he became director of Italian Youth for Catholic

Action, a post he occupied until his abrupt resignation in 1954 and subsequent retreat to the desert.

What was he seeking? Certainly there was an element of discomfort with the conservative political tendencies of Catholic Action in the postwar period. But there was more. On a deeper level he had become disillusioned with big movements, loud rallies, and activism — even on behalf of the Church — that were not sustained by an attitude of prayer and an openness to silence. In a revealing address to his fellow organizers of Catholic Action in 1953 (included as an appendix in *The Desert Journal*), he reflected on "the temptations of the apostolate":

> When the devil is dealing with an executive of Catholic Action, he is wasting his time if he tries to invent ways of making him back down, or raise doubts about his faith which would make him leave Catholic Youth and the Church. Instead of tempting us by pulling us back, he does so by hurrying us forward along the path we are best cut out for. Many temptations passed before my eyes, from the joy of hearing people talk about social programs, to the pleasure of listening to a sermon, until I came to my personal temptations: organizing things, for example, pressing ahead without stopping, and believing in those things as if the salvation of souls depended on them; so it turns into a never-ending race which eventually becomes a torment.

At least as far he was concerned, Carretto was ready to quit that race, to seek and serve God in a different way.

Two of Carretto's posthumously published books, *The Desert Journal*, written during the year of his novitiate, and *Letters to Dolcidia*, his wonderfully affectionate letters to his sister, offer an intimate portrait of his initial encounter with the desert. Carretto was overwhelmed by the oceans of sand, the heat of the day and the surprising cold of the night, the open sky with its canopy of stars (by which he learned to navigate in the dark).

After many years in the public spotlight he luxuriated in the routine of menial labor and the still atmosphere of prayer that nourished his soul. From El Abiodh come the first letters to his family: "*I'm happy, happy, happy,*" he exults, with all the enthusiasm of a boy scout, relishing each detail of the harsh environment and the spartan discipline of the Little Brothers.

But if the desert was a place to encounter God, it was also a place of testing. Soon after his arrival, an accident involving an improperly administered injection in his leg left Carretto crippled for life. At one time an avid outdoorsman, who had dreamed of serving as a Little Brother among Alpine rescue teams, now Carretto faithfully struggled to find God's will in these circumstances, and to identify more compassionately with the suffering of others. According to René Voillaume, "For Carlo, this paralysis was a real and mysterious visitation from God. It was like Jacob being touched on the hip by the angel after a night of wrestling with God." (Carretto's reflections on this experience and its mysterious meaning may be found in his moving book, *Why O Lord?*)

At the same time, other lessons came from his friends and neighbors in the desert — the ex-slaves, the nomads, the impoverished beggars who so often served unwittingly as his guides in faith, hope, charity — and humility. Often Carretto returned to a poignant memory: his failure to give an extra blanket to a shivering beggar, and the subsequent day spent huddled in the shade of a precarious rock, meditating on his lack of charity. In this memory, the desolate desert was no longer a paradise of solitude, but an image of purgatory, reminding him that every circumstance, no matter how unforeseen, and every person, no matter how poor, harbors an invitation to communion with God. Thereon hangs our destiny and the meaning of our lives.

But the most important lesson Carretto learned in the Sahara was that nothing was to be gained from the search for God in the desert if it did not make it easier to find God in the midst of one's fellow human beings. This too had been Foucauld's ideal, to exemplify the intimate connection between the love of God and neighbor, to become, in his phrase, the "Brother of God and the Brother of Men." Thus, in 1964 Carretto left the Sahara and returned to Europe. By that time he knew how to bring the desert with him.

In 1965 he was asked to oversee a new experimental community, the Fraternity of St. Jerome, in Spello, Italy. By this time Carretto had asked to transfer to the Little Brothers of the Gospel, an offshoot of the Little Brothers of Jesus — still inspired by the spirit of Foucauld, but with a somewhat greater openness to apostolic work. His new home was in the Umbrian hills near Assisi and Norcia. In Spello, amid verdant hills and ancient olive groves, the Little Brothers had established a network of hermitages where lay people were invited to share, on a temporary basis, the fraternity's life of prayer and reflection. In these "hills of hope," as Carretto called them, thousands of men and women over time were drawn to taste the spirituality of Charles de Foucauld in the landscape that had inspired both St. Francis and St. Benedict. Describing Spello, Carretto wrote:

> Experience, first matured in action, then in the desert, has shown me the importance of oases of light such as this, where believers can go to live the mystery of the Church; for the Church doesn't live in the desert, and, although having her roots there, must have a place to welcome those who come in from the world bearing all the wounds the world can inflict and who, in the course of the daily solidarity march, have constant need of renewal if they are to remain faithful to the Absolute.

It was in Spello, through his popular retreats and writings, that Carretto acquired his wide following. After *Letters from the Desert* there came a series of titles, including *Love Is for Living, The God Who Comes,* and *In Search of the Beyond,* each in simple words encouraging a thirst for the Transcendent and a life of prayerful love. In *Summoned by Love* he offered a series of meditations on Charles de Foucauld's famous Prayer of Abandonment, while in *Blessed Are You Who Believed* he reflected poignantly on the Mother of God. *I Sought and I Found* was his most autobiographical work, which also contained his most outspoken assessment of the Church and the world.

In leaving Catholic Action Carretto had abandoned the role of the professional activist. But he never ceased to be an active, critical, and even controversial son of the Church. Always opposed to the Church's attraction to pomp and privilege, he joyfully welcomed the fresh air of Vatican II and the promise of a humbler, poorer, servant Church, a community that might better reflect the visage of its divine founder.

At the time of the Vatican Council one of the bishops, in a famous speech, decried the Church's tendency to Triumphalism, Juridicism, and Clericalism. These labels might have served as subheads in Carretto's own lover's quarrel with the Church. He deplored the pretension of the Church to exercise any authority beyond that of love. Christians must strive to become the "brothers and sisters" of all, teaching by example and the purity of their ideals. Thus, he scandalized many of the faithful, including the members of his own family, by supporting the repeal of a ban on civil divorce in Italy. It was not that he lacked sufficient respect for the sacrament of marriage, but that his respect for freedom of conscience convinced him it was wrong to impose the Church's ideals and values on nonbelievers.

The juridical spirit that Carretto opposed was the joyless bondage to law and tradition. Such an attitude stifled the presence of the Holy Spirit, which blows where it will, invigorating the People of God and opening them to the possibility of new life. Part of the value of the desert experience was its capacity to strip one of everything nonessential and to liberate one's heart to receive the gospel of love.

As for clericalism, throughout his life Carretto consciously remained a lay brother, always affirming the dignity of the laity, the "small church of the family" (the title of his first book, published in 1945), and the priesthood of all believers. He spoke frankly about his sorrow that Canon Law proscribed the ordination of married men, thus not only depriving the community of many authentic vocations but in many cases denying them access to the Eucharist itself.

These and similar stands earned him a certain notoriety in Italy and the displeasure of many ecclesiastical authorities. But for all his criticisms there was never any doubt of his loyalty to and love for the Church. He was incredulous at any suggestion that the Church's failures and sins might be a reason for abandoning it. After all, a church without blame or stain would scarcely offer a home and refuge for sinners. Yes, he believed, the Church must strive for holiness, but it is always easier to hold others accountable than it is to strive after holiness ourselves: "No," he wrote, "I shall not leave this Church, founded on so frail a rock, because I should be founding another one on an even frailer rock: myself."

Carretto's attitude toward the Church was one of many points he shared with his favorite saint, Francis of Assisi, whose spirituality he readily imbibed from his Umbrian surroundings. In his playfulness, his appreciation for natural beauty, his commitment to poverty and nonviolence, and in his anarchistic suspicion of large structures and institutions, Carretto clearly identified with the Poverello. It was not by chance that one of his most popular books was the charming *I, Francis,* a personal assessment of the Church and the world delivered in the "voice" of St. Francis. In this book he levels a critique of nearly every feature of modern life — its ugliness, the cult of efficiency and success, the culture of avarice, the commercial degradation of love. At the same time, as in all his books, there is an immense spirit of hope, an ingenuous vitality undiminished by age and illness, and even approaching death.

His last book, written during his final illness and published posthumously, was his most innocently hopeful of all: *And*

God Saw That It Was Good, a kind of love letter from God to the human race. With appropriate timing, Carlo Carretto passed from this life on the feast of St. Francis of Assisi, October 4, 1988. Unlike Charles de Foucauld, murdered alone in the desert, Carretto at seventy-eight died peacefully, after a long illness, and attended by hundreds of friends. But it can be said of both that all their lives were a rehearsal for the end. For Carlo, as for Charles, death was not the final word, but merely the transit to eternity. Indeed, Carlo often drew on the analogy of a child in its mother's womb: we hear our mother's heartbeat and perceive that there is a wider reality beyond our senses, but only by faith can we begin to imagine the life to come.

As with Charles de Foucauld, the reverberations from Brother Carlo's life and writings have extended far and wide. It is hoped that this selection from his writings will capture his essential message and give an account for his wide popularity.

Carlo Carretto represented an ascetic, yet joy-filled spirituality available to lay people, even in the midst of pressing obligations, even amid the din of city noise, even in the midst of poverty and suffering. He showed that a life of prayer need not — indeed must not — relieve us of a passion for social justice and a spirit of solidarity with the least of our brothers and sisters. At the same time he reminded social activists that in the midst of their good works they must preserve a place of stillness, a place where they can listen to the word of God and find renewal. Essentially Carretto showed that it was possible to live a contemplative life in the midst of the world; the desert, after all, is really everywhere. The heart of the gospel is to make of ourselves an oasis of love in whatever desert we might find ourselves. That was the challenge of his life, and it is the ultimate message of this book.

CARLO
CARRETTO

1

I, Carlo

FIRST EXPERIENCE OF LIFE

I was born in Alessandria by...well, you might say, by accident. The city had no connection with my family. We had our true stock, our deep roots, in the Langhe hills, where my father and mother were farmers, with all the sweetness, strength, and piety of that marvelous country in their blood.

But Alessandria became my parents' temporary moorings. Young marrieds then, they had left their home to find employment. They had left behind them the rural civilization in which, God be thanked, they had rejoiced for generations and generations — and which they still carried with them, along with the few household goods to which they had fallen heir from their parents, who had remained up there in the old hamlet, to fade sweetly away like the light of an autumn sunset.

I should like to say something about this young family's displacement. It is something that comes to my mind whenever I think of the numberless such migrations occasioned by unemployment, need, or at times by unforeseen cataclysms like floods or earthquakes.

My father told me the story. He told me how devastating the year had been for the countryside — how hail had fallen with unheard-of violence for that part of the country, destroying everything. The worst was that the disaster had not come in August, when hail was fairly usual in the Langhe region and would batter only the vineyards then. But it had come in June, when not only are the vines vulnerable, but the harvest is standing in the fields.

In short, that year the hail had destroyed absolutely everything: grain and grape, maize and greens.

Nothing was left.

My father told me how the young people of the countryside, in the face of this disaster, had met together and decided to go down to the plains in search of work. They knew that the harvest there required a great many hands, and that they would quickly find work.

He told me — I can still hear his voice — "We left in the evening, and walked all night — the whole forty miles — down to the plain, where farms were big and work was plenty."

The vision of that platoon of youth has remained stamped in my mind — young people refusing to yield to adversity, striding in hope toward a toilsome, tough tomorrow.

I remember, as if it were today, the expression on my father's face; and he added: "Just think, Carlo — after hiking the whole night long, we started reaping in the fields next morning as if we had been peacefully in our beds all night."

That is the way to go, boys and girls!

I remember I looked at my father with admiration. I felt him close to me — and great, precisely in the function of a father, who, by telling the story of his own hard past, had imparted to me something very important: a sense of courage and hope.

My father had not asked himself whether God could exist if he was able to ignore human suffering, or was so distracted and insensitive as to permit cataclysms and hailstorms to pound down on the heads of the poor.

No, he had not wondered about that. For him, and for my mother, the God that existed was the God of hope — the God who made you get on your feet again, out of the rubble of the earthquake, the God who pushed you, impoverished by the scourge of the hail, to begin over again without any fuss, and force yourself to find inside yourself the strength to start out down the road again — and not look to others for everything as if they owed it to you — but above all to free yourself from the bitterness that seeing injustice can give you, or from the surprise of not being helped.

The God of my father was the God of life, the presence always present, always alive and operating within one.

He was the God who does not give you permission to fling yourself on the ground in despair and say, "It's all over!"

It is not true that it is all over. It all changes. And you had better be ready, willing, and able when the change comes, even if it presents itself to you as something hard — and especially if it presents itself to you as something incomprehensible. Who knows? Perhaps this change, this novelty, can bring you something good!

After all . . .

After all, the new, the unforeseeable, has always been the product of disaster.

And this was certainly no small factor in my family's story.

You see, my father ended his story by explaining that this misfortune had so shaken him that he took it into his head to leave his native countryside and go looking for work somewhere else.

He spoke to my mother and she agreed.

He took an examination, and qualified for a job with the State Railways. That was how we landed in Alessandria, where I was born, and where two years later my brother was born. But then we headed for Turin, in search of more suitable surroundings for poor people to rear their adolescent children. We set up house in an outlying, lively district of the city, where there was a little bit of everything, but especially a little bit of everything we needed.

The hail had been a misfortune. That was a fact. But it was also a fact that the hail was why we landed in this quarter, where we were lucky in making many young friends and

where — and this was the height of good luck for us — there
was a little oratory of Don Bosco.

How much that oratory meant to us!

How much it meant to my mother to have that little church
on Via Piazza, where she went to pray and gather strength!

Herein is contained the mystery of the history of our salvation — the mystery of our continual exoduses, of this constant
getting up and moving out, invited and impelled by a force
which, when we do not recognize it, we call fate, but which,
when we are clear about it, and aware, we call the will
of God.

Do you believe that everything is part of a plan, a design, an
intervention of God in our affairs? I do. And I am convinced
that God's love can transform the darkness of a disaster or
the irrationality of an earthquake into an event that can influence, or even completely change, our lives. Ours was certainly
changed. And for the better.

Finding ourselves, in adolescence, in a place so conducive
to the development of our faith, and so rich in wonderful encounters, furnished our migrant family with an effective aid to
becoming more socially adult, more open to good.

It was in this very place that my brother's missionary vocation sprang up, and later the religious orientation of my sisters,
leading both of them to veil and vows.

Years later, when I was studying philosophy, I came upon this
passage in Augustine: "God can permit evil only insofar as he is
capable of transforming it into a good." And in the light or my
own experience, I turned my father's story over in my mind.

And then Augustine's saying seemed to me all the truer.

My family was Christian. That was a fact. I was born to the
faith in this family. I learned to pray at my mother's knee, to
fear God, to go to church, not to blaspheme, to join in the
processions, and to put up the crib when Christmas drew near.

When I think of my childhood piety, traditional, rather static, and somewhat lacking in creative thrust, I still cannot help but find extremely worthwhile values.

Even today I am struck by the unity that faith and culture, the human and the divine, prayer and peace, Church and family, imagination and reality, God and humanity, produced in me.

I had not as yet read the Book of Genesis, where it tells how God placed the human being in the Garden of Eden, to till it and guard it. Yet I felt myself to be in a garden, within the confines of my own world, of my vocation, and was aware of a relationship with him who strolled beneath the trees of the garden, gradually revealing his invisible presence to me.

I did not as yet know Jeremiah, who tells the story of the potter fashioning his clay, who tirelessly refashions the pot that breaks in his hands, shaping another vessel from the same clay (Jer. 18:1–6). But I did feel myself to be in the hands of a God who continuously refashions us and never tires of changing the plans he has made for us when we resist him with the poverty and fragility of our clay.

Yes, my family helped me lay the foundations of faith and hope. And I feel such gratitude for that Langhe region, where I sucked up life, and where the people of the soil kept the calendar of the saints within easy reach, staking out the seasons with the great religious feasts, knowing how to cast their seed into the furrows while invoking St. Lucy and St. Roch, firm in the certainty of a bond between heaven and earth, between rain and prayer, between the happiness of board and bed and the divine order of things.

We shall never be able to say enough about the importance of a popular piety rooted in the flesh and blood of the poor, and slowly ripened over generations, even though — as is only natural — slightly muddled or tinged with a pinch of superstition, yet ever dominated by and enveloped in an immense, unique and solemn mystery: God....

I had the good fortune to be born among the poor, among the marvelous folk of the countryside, who had simplicity and little-ness kneaded into them. My father and mother were very little. They were just made for believing and hoping. And I found myself with my hand in their hands.

And everything was easier.

How at peace I felt with them, and how serene my child-hood was!

It was like living within a great parable, where God was always at home and I was always with him. If, owing to dis-traction or frivolity, I sometimes forgot him, he always thought of a pain or a mystery to remind me of his presence.

But more than anything else, it was events that, very slowly, molded everything together into one. To be sure, the mystery continued to surround me. In fact it became ever denser as I grew up and sought to understand.

The mystery! What was the mystery? It was like my mother's womb, hugging me all about, containing me and generating me to life, in that so discreet, sweet twilight under her heart.

What could be truer and simpler than a woman's womb, containing a child?

But what could be more mysterious and incomprehensible, if you set yourself to reasoning on the how, the why, and the when?

After a placid, unruffled childhood, lived as it were for free in the bosom of my family, I went through an adolescence marked by the struggle with doubt and by the enfeebling of hope.

Uneasiness was born in me, and the dying away of joy be-came ever more noticeable. I came to know things forbidden, and their mysterious attraction.

My mother started telling me not to turn in on myself so much, and would complain about my selfishness.

On occasion, when looking in the mirror, I discovered my capacity for sarcasm.

In my heart, I revolted more and more. My family had less and less influence over me.

Alone, I was reeling.

And then it was that the Church came to meet me.

As the family is the first great aid and support of our first steps, so the Church is the aid and support of all our steps, especially in the struggle against evil.

What would the family be without the community formed by the Church?

What would Israel be without the people of God?

Someone once made a very true and intelligent observation: "You will find peoples without city walls, and without art. But you will never find a people without a temple."

My own first temple was the parish church, which welcomed the big boy I was, the teenager in crisis, the little one in evolution, like an antenna receiving signals from all the beautiful and not so beautiful realities of street, school, factory, shops — from the human community in which I was immersed.

How extraordinary the parish church is! Even when it is a twisted, poor, old-fashioned house as mine was!

We had not reached the Council yet, and the parish church was still a sacrament-dispensing machine and a big hodgepodge of childishness and clericalism.

But it was the meeting place of the people of God, and what human beings did not do, the power of the Spirit and common faith did.

I may have had little faith, but the faith of others met me along the way; unedifying examples there may have been in abundance, but the great examples of the poor, of the simple, and of the holy priests, were never lacking.

How I loved and love the parish church, even though I often hid myself behind the pillars supporting the nave in order to avoid my responsibilities.

The parish church is like a ship at sea, a calm in the woods, a shelter in the mountains. It has always something to offer, even when old and often without form or beauty.

I breathed a tradition, even if a little musty; I absorbed a culture, a bit static though it may have been; I found a people, even if they were sometimes rather tired....

In my own case, the little church that helped me understand the big Church and remain in it, was the Youth Movement of Catholic Action.

It took me by the hand and walked with me, it fed me with the Word, it offered me friendship, it taught me how to fight, it helped me know Christ, it inserted me alive into a living reality.

I can say — and this seems to me to be the correct way of putting it — that just as the family was the spring, so the little youth community was the riverbed in which I learned to swim.

What a help this community was to me!

And what would have become of me if I had not found it?

I tremble at the very thought.

It gave me just what my parents, who were growing old now, could no longer give me....

Catholic Action made me undergo a new catechesis: a more mature one, more in keeping with the times. It passed on to me the great idea of the lay apostolate; it introduced the Church to me as the people of God and not as the familiar, old-fashioned clerical pyramid.

But even more, it gave me the feeling and warmth of community.

For me, the Church was no longer the walls of the parish church, where you went to do obligatory or official things, but a community of brothers known to one another by name, who were traveling with me along the road of faith and love.

There I came to know friendship based on common faith, and commitment to a common task that was no longer the prerogative of the clergy but a gift given to all. I came to know the dignity of working and raising a family as a genuine vocation.

Little by little the community helped me to take on my responsibilities, suggested to me my first commitments and encouraged me in them, taught me how to publish newsletters and write in defense of the faith, and gave me a taste for the Word and taught me to proclaim it at meetings.

And, since I was untrained, the community was always careful to instill in me the humility of study and daily meditation on the Scriptures.

After a few years I found I had changed. Now my heart was filled with new values and a great desire for action.

I remember, there was no more spare time. Between personal contacts and first drafts of speeches, between writing and traveling, my entire personality was caught up, completely caught up, in an ideal that had now taken flesh in real life....

When I was twenty-three and God burst in on me with his Spirit, my new relationship with him radically changed my life.

Everything was new now and everything was influenced by the change that followed my conversion....

The intimacy God bestowed on me was so true, so strong, that it left its tokens and left them where there could be no room for doubt: in life, in sorrow, in joy, in conversation with my fellow-men, in the raw task of every day.

If he held me in his arms, I could spend the whole night in prayer. If he spoke to me, it was easy to forgive someone who had done me wrong. If he stopped in my room, I would have gone to the ends of the earth for the gospel he preached. I shall never forget the manner in which his Spirit burst in on me. He stormed in like someone madly in love and asked me to love him back with total madness of my own.

And there was something here that removed all doubt, that wiped out my suspicion that the encounter could be mere emotionalism, that convinced me that this was for real, and that this tremendous love was something altogether different from fantasy — that it was the Word of God.

In the Word, I found all that I had felt, explained. I found the key to the wonderful castle which I had now entered, without knowing how.

I learned Hosea by heart. With Ezekiel, I wept for my betrayals of love. I hoped against hope with Isaiah, and my story took flesh in the story of Israel....

I was then thinking about getting married: the thought had not even occurred to me that there might be any other choice. I wanted to get married, I dreamed of getting married, I was happy when I thought about being married.

And instead....

It happened one afternoon. It was hot on account of the sirocco blowing across the city.

I was kept waiting by a doctor friend of mine, who was held up at the hospital. We had planned to go for a walk along the Po and talk about our common ideals for changing the world — immediately ... as happens when you are young and still unaware of the actual problems.

I went into a church to calm the tumultuous thoughts burning inside me and sat down quite close to the tabernacle. I felt the refreshing coolness filling the great nave, but closed my eyes because everything was ugly, old, and slovenly. For some time then I had been in the habit of keeping my eyes closed when I prayed, and seeking more for peace than words, more for the Presence than formal worship.

There I was, sitting, when...

Yes, when the unforeseeable happened.

I had often read in the Bible about Abraham's encounter at the terebinth of Mamre.

Was my encounter of the same nature?

I do not know.

Did I recall the burning bush seen by Moses?

Was it the same thing?

I cannot tell....

I had often thought of the touch of Someone who knocks on your door, calling your name, as happened to Samuel, and you feel like saying "Lord, what can I do for you?"

It was like this, but different—impossible to put such things into words. I know that this unforeseeable "passage" left me with something very clearly and precisely new: an altogether unfamiliar proposal, the beginning of a personal, particularly challenging, and warm conversation.

You will not marry.

You will stay single.

I shall be with you.

Do not be afraid.

In the days that followed, it was easy to see that things had changed in me and that the passage of God had been a radical one. I had the palpable conviction that I would now no longer be able to fall in love in a certain way with a woman, and that if I wanted to be happy, I should have to remain single.

Alone with my God.   —*I Sought and I Found*

THE MYSTERY OF A CALLING

God's call is mysterious; it comes in the darkness of faith. It is so fine, so subtle, that it is only with the deepest silence within us that we can hear it.

And yet nothing is so decisive and overpowering for a person on this earth, nothing surer or stronger.

This call is uninterrupted: God is always calling us! But there are distinctive moments in this call of his, moments which leave a permanent mark on us—moments which we never forget.

Three times in my life I have been aware of this call.

The first one brought about my conversion when I was eighteen years old. I was a schoolteacher in a country village.

In Lent a mission came to the town. I attended it, but what I remember most of all was how boring and outdated the sermons were. It certainly wasn't the words which shook my state of apathy and sin. But when I knelt before an old missionary — I remember how direct his look was and how simple — I was aware that God was moving in the silence of my soul.

From that day on I knew I was a Christian and was aware that a completely new life had been opened up for me.

The second time, when I was twenty-three, I was thinking of getting married. It never occurred to me that I should do anything else.

I met a doctor who spoke to me of the Church and of the beauty of serving her with one's whole being, while remaining in the world. I do not know what happened at that time nor how it happened; the fact is that I was praying in an empty church where I had gone to escape from my state of inner confusion. I heard the same voice that I had heard during my confession with the old missionary. "Marriage is not for you. You will offer your life to me. I shall be your Lover forever."

I had no difficulty in giving up the idea of getting married and consecrating myself to God because everything within me was changed. It would have seemed incongruous to me, falling in love with a girl, for God engaged my whole life.

Those years were full of work, of aspirations, of meeting different people, and of wild dreams. Even the mistakes — and there were many — were caused by the fact that so much within me was still unpurified.

Many years passed; and many times I was amazed to find myself praying to hear once more the sound of that voice which had had so great an importance for me.

Then, when I was forty-four years old, there occurred the most serious call of my life: the call to the contemplative life. I experienced it deeply in the depth which only faith can provide and where darkness is absolute — where human strength can no longer help.

This time I had to say "yes" without understanding a thing. "Leave everything and come with me into the desert. It is not your acts and deeds that I want; I want your prayer, your love."

Some people, seeing me leave for Africa, thought that I must have had some personal crisis, some disappointment. Nothing is further from the truth. By nature I am optimistic, my orientation is one of hope; and I don't know the meaning of discouragement and it would never occur to me to "give up the fight" in this way.

No, it was the decisive call. And I never understood it so deeply as on that evening at the Vespers of St. Charles in 1954, when I said "yes" to the voice.

"Come with me into the desert." There is something much greater than human action: prayer; and it has a power much stronger than human words.

And I went into the desert.

Without having read the constitutions of the Little Brothers of Jesus I entered their congregation. Without knowing Charles de Foucauld* I began to follow him.

For me it was enough to have heard the voice say to me, "This is the way for you."

Wandering among the desert tracks with the Little Brothers I discovered how real that way was. By following Charles de Foucauld, I was convinced that it was the way for me.

God had already told me that in faith.

When I reached El Abiodh Sidi Seik for the novitiate, my novice master told me with the perfect calm of a man who had lived twenty years in the desert: *"Il faut faire une coupure,*

---

*Charles de Foucauld (1858–1916) was born into an aristocratic family, but after a dissolute youth he pursued a spiritual path that led him ultimately to the Saharan desert, where he sought to imitate the "hidden" life of Jesus of Nazareth. Ordained a priest in 1901, he established his first hermitage in Béni-Abbès in Algeria, later moving to Tamanrasset, where he was killed on December 1, 1916. Seventeen years after his death his life and writings inspired René Voillaume, a French priest, to establish the Little Brothers of Jesus, the first of several congregations linked in their origins to the spirituality of Foucauld.

Carlo." I knew what kind of cutting he was talking about and decided to make the wrench, even if it were painful.

In my bag I had kept a thick notebook, containing the addresses of my old friends: there were thousands of them. In his goodness God had never left me without the joys of friendship.

If there was one thing I really regretted when I left for Africa, it was not being able to speak to each one of them, to explain the reason for my abandoning them, to say that I was obeying a call from God and that, even if in a different way, I would continue to fight on with them to work for the kingdom.

But it was necessary to make the "cut" and it demanded courage and great faith in God.

I took the address book, which for me was the last tie with the past, and burned it behind a dune during a day's retreat.

I can still see the black ashes of the notebook being swept away into the distance by the wind of the Sahara.

But burning an address is not the same thing as destroying a friendship, for that I never intended to do; on the contrary, I have never loved nor prayed so much for my old friends as in the solitude of the desert. I saw their faces, I felt their problems, their sufferings, sharpened by the distance between us.

For me they had become a flock which would always belong to me and which I must lead daily to the fountains of prayer.

Sometimes I almost felt their physical presence when, for example, I entered the Arab-style church at El Abiodh or, later, the famous hermitage constructed by Fr. Charles de Foucauld himself at Tamanrasset.

Prayer had become the most important thing. But it was still the hardest part of my daily life. Through my vocation to prayer I learned what is meant by "carrying other people" in our prayer.

So, after many years I can say that I have remained true to my vocation, and at the same time I am completely convinced that one never wastes one's time by praying; there is no more helpful way of helping those we love.   — *Letters from the Desert*

TO THE DESERT

Marseilles-Orano, December 11, 1954

My dearest Sister,*

I'm writing to you because *I know you're very concerned* and because I think I'll catch you at this very moment in church, praying for your brother who's going away.

Poor Dolce! The Lord has given you the vocation of holding in your heart all the cares of the family. And of suffering them.

Don't worry, Dolce; it's God who's calling me. I know his voice. Think of my life up till now: I've always followed the right star, haven't I? Haven't I pulled in great netsful of souls? But I couldn't rest on my laurels anymore: my capital was all used up. I would have ended up a mediocre representative for God, dissatisfied with myself. There was nothing for it but to make a break, and since God said "come," I had the courage (by his grace) to respond. Just think: I'm sailing the same African sea as St. Augustine: over there is his diocese of Hippo.

I'm going into the *desert*, my desert. Even if I'm making a mistake and have to return (but I don't think so), I can't imagine anything better than a year's *desert*, real desert. I want to empty myself and become nothing, then say to Jesus: fill me with Yourself alone.

Isn't that a grace? Be happy. You know I've always been shrewd and made good deals. I've never made such a good deal as this.

How often we have discussed the sterility of today's apostolate. I want to go and study the real thing, because this is the best situation and the best place to understand how useless the superstructures are.

---

*This was the first letter written by Carretto after his departure from Rome. It is addressed to his sister Dolcidia, a nun in the Institute of the Daughters of Mary Help of Christians in Turin.

And after all, you will pray for me: You won't abandon me to my loneliness, will you?

I'm so happy, Dolce! I feel as though I'm fifteen and just starting out. It will be the sweetest novitiate of my life, made in the place where the Desert Fathers made theirs, in the biblical footsteps of the real mystics of the past, those who laid the foundations of European Christianity.

What an immense grace God is giving me! But how did I come to deserve it after so many sins? Truly our God is a God of mercy! He loads you with gifts at the very time you're giving him no thought, or worse, betraying him.

He is Father!

And I want to become his son, his real son.

He is Jesus my brother.

And I want to become a genuine brother to him.

He is the Spirit of Love.

And I want to enroll in his School of Fire and let myself be all burnt up.

What a joy, my dear sister!

I send you such a hug as I've never given you in my life, because I love you as never before.

                                                          Love, Carlo

•

                                          El Abiodh, December 16, 1954
Dearest Dolce, dearest all,

Here I am settled in the peace of the African desert. Today dawn broke on my first morning as a novice after a night under the stars.

Let's go back and tell the story in the right order. As you well know, I left Termini on the evening of the Immaculate Conception after a quiet night, and reached Marseilles in pouring rain. . . .

On the morning of the 11th I went aboard the *Bel-Abbes,* a ferry of almost ten thousand tons, after saying goodbye to the friends who had come with me. The crossing was good despite a rather choppy sea and...headlong dashes by some of the passengers, especially the ladies. A day later, or to be exact at one o'clock on Sunday the 12th, I set foot on African soil at the port of Orano. Here too I was expected and spent Sunday afternoon at Mass in the cathedral and visiting this beautiful African city. On Monday morning I journeyed on southward in a coach bound for Jaida, passing through the fertile Algerian coastal strip.

It was wonderful arable land, just as well cultivated as the most fertile lands of Europe. Vines, olives, fruit trees, oranges, mandarins, wheat: everything that a Mediterranean country can produce. And the early spring vegetables like peas and so on were fully ripe.

After Jaida I took another coach for Géryville, the first leg of my long journey. Here, little by little as I moved on, the vines decreased and the rocks and cold increased, a sure sign that the sea's kindly influence was falling behind me. I arrived at Géryville in the afternoon as guest of the White Fathers, where I was received, as everywhere, with much warmth. I spent the night in Géryville with...a stove burning in my room (this tells you that the Sahara is a very cold land which gets hot when the sun shines). In the morning I was lucky enough to find the sun shining so that I could leave again for the South (when it rains, and in winter it rains a lot in this first stretch of steppe, nobody leaves because the tracks are flooded with water and impossible to travel). So I set off in a sturdy truck, with which to tackle the hardest 60-odd miles (after the 250 already traveled).

Bear it in mind that it took me almost six hours, seeing that we had to travel very very slowly along impossible tracks through the steppe. The steppe isn't yet desert, but a preparation for it. Imagine a vast plateau at more than three thousand feet strewn with rocks, sand, clumps of grass as tough as steel blades, and here and there nomad Bedouins' herds of sheep and camels.

Toward the end of the journey the steppe stopped and the real desert began. In fact, El Abiodh is the last center of habitation before the wide open Sahara, a real sea of sand with just a few oases where water bubbles up.

I arrived at 3:00 p.m. to be met with great eagerness by about forty French, Belgian, Peruvian, Spanish, and Canadian novices (just about the whole world in fact), and particularly by Fr. [Arturo] Paoli, who was here, dressed as a novice.

El Abiodh is a tiny but very beautiful oasis. It consists of an Arab-style building, which includes a church and some porticoes, off of which open the cells. A community of about fifty Little Brothers lives here, dedicating themselves to manual labor and prayer. They make bread and till the fields (the few possible), build walls, make household objects, and live as the poorest of the poor.

All possessions are held in common, and there are no aesthetic considerations (I've still got things to learn). We eat sitting on the floor in the dining room off a single aluminum plate. We drink water out of the one jug and anyone who is squeamish can leave within the day. In the cells we sleep on the floor (there are no beds) and everything is reduced to the indispensable minimum.

The whole thing recalls the original Franciscans, but the local atmosphere is an Arab one of the greatest simplicity possible to imagine. It really is a complete stripping away! And it is just this which leads to the most complete feeling of freedom and joy. Around me I see nothing but happy faces oozing joy at every pore.

They are Spartans in training for a really hard life. This is our timetable: rise at 3:00 a.m., for prayers until 7:00.

Begin work at, 7:00 which lasts until 1:00 p.m. Builders, farm-workers, carpenters, electricians, truck-drivers, etc. They work on the house, they build the women's novitiate a few hundred yards away, and they make all the craft objects for the surrounding Arab villages. In the afternoon, adoration of the Blessed Sacrament, study, and a bit more work.

At 9:00 we go off to sleep or to write letters. After 11:00 we all have to be in our beds, which are not beds, because we sleep on the floor on a mat. The nights are as cold as in our mountains, and the days are hot. The same thing happens here as in our mountains, where there is an extraordinary difference between when the sun is shining and when it's not. We go from a few degrees Fahrenheit below freezing to 85 above. They say that in summer it goes from a few degrees above freezing to 110 above in the sun.

We shall see. At the moment it's winter and comfortable. I have been given a cell of my own, which is seen as a mark of respect, but I don't think it will last long because novices continue to arrive and there's no more space.

I have fallen in with some amazing people. They are all used to tough spiritual battles and, like us, have made headway in them. No young person is taken on before the age of twenty and I think I understand the reason. You and Emerenziana,* who did ordinary novitiates, have no idea of what things are like here. Nobody thinks about material things. There is almost a couldn't-care-less attitude toward all comfort and a search for austerity.

But it's all about prayer, and the hours of adoration feel like communal battles. *The silence is infinite,* and the desert which surrounds this oasis is forever inviting us to keep quiet. This is really the most solemn impression I have had since my arrival.

I don't yet know what I shall be doing: perhaps they will make me a builder or a fieldworker because I am sturdy. It is the Trappist rule: seven hours work, seven hours prayer, and seven or less of sleep.

---

*Carretto's oldest sister, Emerenziana, was also, like Dolcidia, a member of the Daughters of Mary Help of Christians.

You can imagine how happy I feel! Really happy! I've received an infinite grace from the Lord and I've got to be worthy
of it. Don't worry. I wrote to you, Dolcidia, *that I have always
found my guiding star. I feel I've found it this time too.*

God loves me like a baby and is guiding me like a child.
Don't worry. *Instead pray for me as much as you can....*

Lots of kisses, Carlo

•

El Abiodh-Sidi-Sheikh, Christmas 1954
Dearest Dolcidia, dearest all,

The Christmas star of 1954 has led me into the great Sahara
desert in the footsteps of Fr. de Foucauld.

El Abiodh, which is where I am living at the moment, is a
tiny oasis perched on the edge of the great sea of sand, which
stretches south as far as Equatorial Africa. It is made up of two
little Arab villages built out of sun-dried brick, in which the
population lives barricaded around a few wells, committed to
tending herds and cultivating a few little fields of corn. Next
to the two villages stands the novitiate of the "Little Brothers
of Jesus," of which Fr. de Foucauld dreamed and for which he
wrote the Rule; Fr. Voillaume, the author of the book *Seeds of
the Desert,* organized it with a few companions.

The first thing that strikes you when you come to El Abiodh
is the silence. It is an immense, total, all-absorbing silence. The
last sixty-two miles of steppe, over a poor road even for trucks,
are a good preparation for this African setting of stark horizons,
nomad herdsmen, and sand battling against the last clumps of
grass and thorns.

It would certainly be difficult to find a place more suited to
meditation and adoration, and we can see at once why Fr. de
Foucauld, who was called the last Desert Father, said this place
had a particular power to call distracted and sensual souls back
to God.

The nomads' black tents (symbol of the human journey toward the Eternal Pastures), the Arabs prostrate in prayer, the luminosity of the sky (European eyes are not used to this), the great sea of sand that surrounds us, the inescapable realities of silence and death — these are indisputably the elements of an ascetical life. In this place the novice master's invitation seems natural: divest yourself totally of all you had until yesterday — clothes, suitcases, boxes, nips of drinks, dabs of scent, hidden comforts — while you repeat to yourself: *Take no more care for your life and health than for a tree or a falling leaf.*

Once stripped naked you are reclothed in workman's clothes, which are not your own, and a white Arab "gandura" which you will use in church during choir. That is the way your life begins, as a pupil of a Desert Father.

You get a mat on the ground, a sleeping bag into which you climb on cold nights, a pair of sandals, and a Rule specially designed to bend the stiffest backs like mine. It could be summed up more or less as: seven hours manual labor, seven hours prayer, and seven hours sleep.

This is what is needed for this band of forty French, Belgian, African, Chilean, Spanish, and Brazilian novices. They have all, like me, reached adulthood, been tested in battle and infected by the "problematic" and by "cultural indoctrination" of a religious sort. Here the overriding law is: "Stop thinking about what you have to do to win over the brothers; worry about being. From now on your sermon has to be your life and not your words. And living an authentic life means copying the life of Jesus."

Fr. Foucauld was fond of distinguishing three periods in the life of Jesus: Nazareth, the desert, and the public life.

He lived out his Rule on this scheme: To copy Nazareth, seek out solitude to fill yourself with God, burn with love for souls.

1. *Nazareth.* To achieve the imitation of Jesus of Nazareth, you accept being poor laborers for the whole of your life. This is a major effort, especially for those of us who come from the

middle class. The set-up of the novitiate, and of the Brotherhood where we will go to live later, is based on work. The
vow of poverty accepts the same poverty as laborers and wage-
earners, in a word the people. Moreover, it was the poverty
of Jesus.

Before clothing me in the novice's habit, Fr. Voillaume asked
me, "Are you ready for the Gospel of Jesus, not only to live the
life of a poor man with no possessions, but also to accept the
conditions of the poor, who must work to live, as divine law
requires?"

Once this premise has been stated, the rest falls into place.
Would you like me to give you an idea of how we live? Imagine
a building site along a road under construction. Clothes, food,
medicine, conveniences: they are exactly the same as those imposed by the harsh law of manual labor which is the labor of
the poorest. There is food and enough of it, but it comes in a
mess tin with no refinements. And if you leave any, you eat it
the next evening, and if you still leave some, you eat it the next;
that's what the poor do. Clothes? As tattered and dusty as on
a building site. The infirmary? If you saw it, and its infirmar-
ian, you would understand what I meant before by the saying,
"Don't be more anxious about your own life than about a tree
or a falling leaf."

2. *The desert.* This is certainly one of the marks of the team
which I have joined by becoming a "Little Brother." Here they
are so convinced that the reasons for the "crisis" are within ourselves, in our superficiality, in the very superstructures of our
piety, that they adopt no half-measures to get away from it.
They have to make a clean sweep, and then with the one book
they let you keep, the Bible, they send you out into the solitude
and give the desert the job of getting to work on you. It has to
be experienced to be believed, so much so that I've been convinced right from my first encounter that the Lord created the
desert just to give space to souls needing to collect themselves.

That is why, faced with the dominant paganism of the early centuries, Christianity went to sink its roots in the desert, with the monasticism of East and West.

3. *The apostolic life.* The apostolate of the Little Brothers is directed toward the poor and most forsaken, or better still toward those furthest from Christ, where words are almost useless but witness is necessary. That is why the two great areas toward which we are urged are Islam and the world of work.

What do you preach to a Muslim? It's not just useless; its impossible. What do you preach to workers poisoned by Marxism? It's the same.

What then? You stand alongside them, living as they do, with the witness of a Christian life rich in love and joy despite the pain of labor. When it's necessary one should talk too, but the overriding concern is to demonstrate the goodness of the gospel with one's life.

You can see the power of this formula, which at any rate is the one which has won me over.

You can see why we study Arabic here, and Russian even more so. You have your finger on the pulse of our situation, the situation toward which the modern world is moving, so you won't find it difficult to see the fruitfulness of such an evangelical appeal, launched by a poor hermit in love with God and humanity, such as was Charles de Foucauld.

That is why he left the Trappists.

He saw them to be too removed from people. He reconstituted them on a smaller scale alongside people. He wanted his followers to be Trappists in the midst of the suffering, the poverty, and the insecurity of the poor of our day. He wanted their sole concern to be the love of Christ made present in "permanent prayer" and continual "availability" to people.

But let's leave these things which I put badly and which you can find put well in the book *Seeds of the Desert*. Let's deal with simpler things which I, your brother and friend, can tell you.

To start with, I can tell you that I remember you all. In the long periods of adoration before the Blessed Sacrament — there is always Exposition here after work — your faces and your problems pass one by one through my mind. It is so easy here to remember everybody.

Then I can tell you again that I will pray for you and I shall be happy if you will entrust me with this task, especially for the things that are hardest and most burdensome for you. In this way I shall feel that I am battling alongside you again just as I used to do.

Forgive me for writing this communal letter. Basically it was a question of making the same introductory remarks, and it went against the grain to waste time repeating them all in a lot of letters.

Later on it won't be like that: it will give me real pleasure to get down to discussing with you matters which are woven deeply into our friendship, and our ideals of love for God and his Church.

Pray for me that I will be faithful to the call of Jesus — imperious as it was — so that I may achieve a life of effective evangelical witness and make up for such a dull and bombastic past.

I carry you with me in all love in my God-filled solitude.

Love, Carlo

•

El Abiodh, January 21, 1955

Dearest Dolce and dear all,

First things first: *I'm happy, happy, happy and I feel like I'm fifteen years old.*

I got the feeling from Sr. Dolcidia's letter that you all (or she) were rather taken aback by the harshness of the life which we lead here. No, don't worry yourselves in the slightest, but believe me genuinely and literally when I say: *I'm happy.* It's true that life here is as tough as it is for those in the mountains, but what does toughness matter? Mountain people enjoy it even when they sleep on a plank floor and eat out of a mess tin, don't they?

The life we lead is Spartan: sleeping on the floor and wearing permanently dirty overalls and not bothering with a tie don't matter...but the whole thing is accepted in such a carefree spirit of joy *that we feel sorry for those who peer into the mirror and worry about the color of their shirt.* The fact is that here we go back to school to *become poor,* and you know that poverty is apparently painful but really nothing less than a beatitude (blessed are the poor) and therefore a source of great, very great joy. What is more, it is a school for *freedom* and *detachment,* both of them divine and marvelous things.

Mamma, don't you worry about what I'm eating: I'm eating very well. To be sure, if you served at home some of the dishes served here...you would hear shrieks and see long faces. Of course there are things to laugh about. The most unthinkable things come out of the kitchen and we have the strangest possible menus. Imagine this for a lunch: starter: soup; main course: pasta; dessert: dates; or another: first course: boiled potatoes; main course: mashed potatoes; dessert: figs.

Now they want me to join the kitchen; I'm sure that even if I prepared the food with my feet I would be a hit. But this doesn't matter, and if I make the pasta too tasty they'll chase me out of the kitchen as a *tempter.*

You see, here we live like real workmen because we have to pick up our trade from the teaching of Jesus of Nazareth. But I wouldn't have believed that I would find so much joy in freeing myself from so much vanity, superficiality, greed, and pretension.

Detachment from things leaves you with such a sense of *freedom!* You don't worry anymore whether you're ugly or handsome, bearded or beardless. Here it's rather almost a competition to get into the worst clothes and get rid of the slavery of middle-class habits (would you believe that I trim my beard once a week, I who used to shave every morning?).

Obviously, all this is not a goal; *it's a means* toward eliminating every form of servitude, toward making us sturdy, toward learning to suffer, to work, *and to become simple because the gospel is for the simple* and is better understood that way.

All the complications of modern life, especially a rich one, are full of poison and, as I see more clearly now, they take people away from the gospel and *make them sad.*

That is the way it is and it is for this very reason that I am so happy.

The Lord *guided me well* and brought me to just the right place, and here I am experiencing my first spiritual benefits.

It's a pity that the time flies so quickly and already more than a month has gone by. I shall have to speed up because I've only a year of testing, and then I shall have to leave the desert and go back among people. A year is so little for backs as stiff as mine.

A few days ago I left the building site and became a farmer. I work with cabbages, potatoes, and salad vegetables. I've harvested the olives, and now I'm pickling them (eleven hundred pounds of olives entrusted to my skills). It's rather like the kitchen being entrusted to certain cooks who come out with soup for starters and pasta as a main course.

The weather is fine but very windy. If you could see the desert when the wind blows! You live in a cloud of sand: you breathe sand, you eat sand, your eyes are full of sand. But we also live here because sand is clean, not dirty. When they do not have water, the Arabs purify themselves before prayer by rubbing their hands and faces with sand; they think of it as water. I haven't yet got that far, but I'm getting there. A few days ago we had a holiday and I used it to make a twenty-mile walk into the desert. I climbed a little mountain from which the whole breadth of the Sahara can be seen. It was marvelous. Enough for now: I'll tell you the rest another time.... Love, Carlo
— *Letters to Dolcidia*

A LITTLE BROTHER

Christmas Day 1955

I am a Little Brother. I buried the old Professor in the caves of the Col at Géryville. Now I am beginning a new life.

The most important feature of my spiritual life is my total renunciation of guiding myself, of concerning myself with and analyzing the procedures of my Christian life. I have relinquished all this to God.

From now on I want to keep my eyes on him, and him alone. He will take care of me. My act of faith must be complete and without second thoughts. Gifts have come for me too, but...I am afraid to open the parcel. We shall see in the days to come.

Works! Houses without the Father, churches without God, kitchens without a fire, bedrooms without love.

Method! Work makes you lose weight; poverty sets you free. So, having become light, you get used to praying. The least that can happen to you is that you take flight. And the desert which stretches away before you — awe-inspiring, silent, infinite — beckons you to seek its heart, where you will be alone, alone with your God.

Working priests and Little Brothers: a pastoral presence and a religious presence.   — *The Desert Journal*

•

El Abiodh, March 1, 1955

Dearest Sr. Dolce and Sr. Emerenziana,

You are sad (and I'm pleased *because it is a sign of love*) that I haven't sent another personal word to the two of you. I'm doing so today because I have a little free time, since the blizzard of sand which has battered the desert for the last few days has rather changed our work schedule. At any rate, thank you for your most affectionate letters, accompanied as I feel they were by much impassioned prayer. *How dear and precious is our family, united as it is by the bond of mutual prayer!* I think that it is difficult to escape that fact, and that the weaknesses of one member are immediately supplied by the prayers of another, and one member's crisis by another's eagerness, so that the whole team marches forward with confidence toward its Homeland. Don't you agree? ...

You are waiting for a word from me, and that's certainly not difficult, especially nowadays that we have put on the same habit, the same discipline: religious life. You will surely want to know my impressions, my feelings about it, and so forth.

Here goes: there is nothing more *holy* or more *oppressive,* more *sublime* or more *stupid,* more *constructive* or more *useless* than the religious life. Everything depends on the spirit with which you tackle it.

The Rule? It can be a stairway to heaven or the most inhuman trap you can imagine. *Now I really understand what Jesus was telling the religious of his time: "The sinners and the tax-collectors will take their places before you!"* For them the religious life was a trap, and it was precisely with that that they killed Jesus. Because remember: the people who killed Jesus were the religious of his time, not the sinners and robbers.

As I was saying, it all depends on the spirit in which it is tackled.

For example, what is poverty, ratified and solemnly confirmed by a vow?

It's like all the other virtues: having within ourselves "the same mind as Jesus, who although his state was divine emptied himself to assume the condition of a slave, and became.... "

What can poverty become for the religious when it is taken on with a vow?

The solution to all financial problems, the absence of all worries, that happy calm in which everything is looked after and tomorrow is taken care of by gilt-edged securities in the bank.

That's the trap. What is there left resembling the drama of Mary and Joseph adrift in a foreign land, *really* poor and worried about where to find a bite of food for Jesus? The same goes for all the rest, and in that rest lies an absolute betrayal of the religious life, the Church, and Christ.

Obedience? It can be a total, unconditional, joyous abandonment to our one King and Master: or it can be a school for cowardice and a priori rejection of the thing that costs a man dearest: personal responsibility. Isn't that so?

So, my dear sisters, I put it to you: given that we've got the experience, we've got the willingness to serve God, do we want in the years left to us to serve God here on Earth, to live out our vocation in depth, to make it a stairway to heaven? Nothing else matters anymore and we ought to burn all our boats behind us. There is no going back. Since we have chosen to be poor, let us live like the poor; since we have accepted virginity, let's live like virgins . . . and not just like single people; since we have accepted God, let us renounce the world.

How the desert speaks of these things to me! The desert, you see, is *just sand and sky. Down below sand which is death, up above a sky which is brighter than anywhere else.* If only you could see the stars here! How they sparkle! Now I understand why the Arabs have not lost their faith as Europeans have and why many European soldiers who came into contact with Arabs came back to God. It's the school of the desert.

When I have a free day, I take a lump of bread and a walking-stick and go off for the whole day. I travel twelve or so miles completely alone in this immense solitude and that way I'm alone with God. It's called *khalna* in Arabic and it means: to go into solitude.

Remember that one of the novitiate tests is to make a month of spiritual exercises like this. We set out and travel about 375 miles (Rome–Turin, more or less) toward Béni-Abbès, the oasis where Fr. Foucauld lived and found his vocation. It's the test of completely emptying one's mind, and they say it is startlingly effective in leading one to repentance and pure faith. When the time comes I'll tell you about it.

At the moment I'm still here, and I work and sing and pray. Above all do I pray. I would like to achieve real intimacy with God and remove the thick veil that divides us and causes my faith to be still so vague and unsure. The route here is the right one: the Blessed Sacrament is exposed almost all day long and the community gravitates toward it.

There is a great insistence here on searching for Jesus as a personal bridge to God. Basically it's the mystery of the Incarnation of the Word, the mystery that comes right up against us and of which we have to make use. There's no news of human affairs. The voice of the world does not get this far, it's all silence....

How nice it would be to see you again. It's strange how love grows here instead of fading away!

A big kiss from your Carlo

●

Assekrem, Christmas 1958

Dearest Dolce,

It's Christmas morning. Last night, after my annual spiritual exercises, I renewed my triennial vows. That means it's four years since I left Rome: one year at El Abiodh and three years divided between Berre and here in the Hoggar.

I'm not going to draw up an account of this period for you because I wouldn't know where to begin and, worse still, where to end. I can only tell you that I have found my way and that I am very happy.

I don't want to give you an apologia for the Little Brothers, and in any case I don't believe in formulae anymore, but I just want to tell you that for four years I've lived in an atmosphere where the gospel strikes a deeper chord, and that is all.

Here I'm left to get on with praying and my superiors are more concerned about my holiness than all my work. In short, I feel that what matters is the search for personal sanctity and union with God, not works.

And that's no small thing for a Congregation.

Yesterday evening a car arrived from Tamanrasset, and I had the joy of receiving your last letter of December 15.

I see that as usual you complain about my silence and I apologize profusely. You're not the only one left to complain about me.

It's strange, but throughout my life I have always found people eager to read what I write. It's really an act of great humility and patience, and I thank them all, but I don't think I will change much.

On the mainland my old friends hunt about for news of me, and I really can't understand why it matters to them. By now I'm a hermit and to a hermit time and space no longer exist. Don't you agree?

I'm not secretary to a mother general; I live in a cave built out of stone and mud and I've little to tell.

The desert is always the same, the sky is always beautiful, the road deserted.

What else can I say?

The only thing which is always new is God, but to talk about him you've got to be a very good and careful secretary and even so you don't always get anything. What's more, he likes to present us with long periods of pure faith during which there's nothing for it but to be silent and strive to love, to love as much as you can with this old and stinking flesh, from which only iniquity and wretchedness can be squeezed.

What would you like to say?

But today my heart is full of Jesus and I could write you a novel. How many things the Lord told me last night! Especially *one* which I want to tell you about immediately.

Do you want the secret of everything? Do you want a boiled-down summary of the gospel? Do you want a tiny, tiny, easy, easy formula for running, for flying onto the road to holiness?

Here it is:

"Strive to love."

I don't tell you to love, because it's not an easy thing. *To love* certain unlikable "Sisters" who are living and getting on alongside us, especially in a big house, is almost impossible. I tell you instead to "strive" to love because translating a precept into action is almost always done *on the Cross*. Nothing which is really good and holy is easy for us. It takes an effort. It is the Cross laid upon our poor hearts and at the touch of it life begins to flow again.

Seek every day — I'm telling you my suggestions from last night — some opportunity to love more both God and neighbor.

What results you'll see!

Jesus expects no more than that.

The whole of the Law and the Prophets is summed up as: *love — love.*

Try it and let me know.

In any case the advice does not come from me but from Jesus himself. Tomorrow I shall come down off the mountain and take to the road again. I think I will carry on working here for the time being. I have asked Fr. Prior if I may spend the rest of my life here, but I don't know what he will do with me....

                                                                    Carlo
                                                    — *Letters to Dolcidia*

LEARNING TO LOVE

When I left for Africa to become a Little Brother of Jesus I lived for some time in Algiers, as the guest of an old friend.

I was very unsettled in those days, and the world appeared to me under quite a new light. It had something to do with that intuition born in the heart of him whom I now wanted to follow along the desert tracks, Charles de Foucauld.

The perspective of a European, materially and culturally endowed, desirous of giving and doing something for others, had turned somersaults in me. I would have liked to hide, without money in my pocket, dressed as an Arab, among the anonymous crowd of poor Muslims seething in the alleys of Kasbah.

I remember that around midday I noticed a long string of men in rags lining up near the convent, whose walls were as solid as a fortress.

Each man had a tin can. I saw a door open and a nun in a white habit appear; nearby was an enormous smoking pot. It was time for the daily distribution of alms, and each man received his share along with a loaf of bread and warm soup.

I stared at that procession as though in a dream; as I watched those men and women branded with misery, tears ran down my cheeks, so that I could no longer see the bright sky above the African city.

I tried to find a place for myself. I had left my native land, urged on by the desire to give up everything in order to give myself to God among all this poverty; to search out among the poor the crucified face of Jesus, to do something for my wretched and despised brethren, so that, by loving them, I might deepen my union with God.

What was I to do then? Was I to open dispensaries and give bread, medicine, and education to these poor people? What was my place in the great evangelizing work of the Church?

I tried to learn from him who had drawn me to Africa, Charles de Foucauld. Quite small, quite humble, tin can in hand, I found him in my imagination, at the end of the queue. He was smiling faintly, as if he wanted to ask pardon for adding himself to the number of the deprived and underprivileged.

Undoubtedly, at that moment, in spite of my fear of suffering, my reluctance to bear the burdens of others, my fear of taking up the cross, I understood that my place, too, was there, amid the ragged poor, mixing in the mob.

Others in the Church would have the task of evangelizing, building, feeding, preaching. The Lord asked me to be a poor man among poor men, a worker among workers.

Yes, above all, a worker among workers, since the world of today was no longer in search of alms as in the time of Francis of Assisi, but a world in search of work, justice, and peace.

The world toward which I was journeying was the world in which real poverty is experienced. For people in that world, work is their sackcloth, but they have not chosen it; moreover it is painful, dirty, and poorly paid.

After a week spent at Taifet I left again for Tamanrasset. I felt that I could not bear that wretchedness and poverty any longer. In this I was poorer than those poor men, for I had been unable to bear what they had always borne.

I needed prayer. I longed to find myself alone in my hermitage where Jesus was exposed day and night, in order to unburden myself to him, beseech him, lose myself in him.

Above all I wanted to ask him to make me smaller, emptier, more transparent — and to enable me to return to Taifet.

Yes, return to Taifet to live the last years of my life. Have a little hut "like them," no possessions but a mat and a blanket, "like them," on the shore of that *oued* [riverbed], drag a little water from it with those *fogaras* which were continually breaking down as though laughing at our labor!

But also to have Jesus in the Host, hidden in the hut; to adore him, pray to him, love him, and obtain from him the strength not to rebel, not to curse, but to accept lovingly what the day would bring.

And so I pray for the day when on the shore of that *oued* a little cross will rise like a sentinel to watch over the solitude of those men as they wait, wait for others to come, and love them and help them to love.   — *Letters from the Desert*

DREAMS, LOST AND FOUND

I'd gone off to Africa and joined the novitiate of the Little Brothers of Jesus at El Abiodh in Algeria.

I went to the Little Brothers of Father de Foucauld in response to a call to consecration heard in my heart and requiring
a clear answer from me.

The idea of giving myself to the last and least of the earth,
the poorest of the poor — the thought of merging myself in the
dough of the world as living leaven — attracted me. I wanted to
devote my existence to others and I wanted to do it where the
going would be tough. The desert would be the perfect place, I
thought. "Present to God, and present to people," was the way
the great mystic of the Sahara Charles de Foucauld put it, and
I wanted to embody those two tensions at unity in a life where
contemplation and action went hand in hand.

And there in the novitiate of the Little Brothers I began to
dream, and dream, and dream.

Do you know what I dreamed about?

I dreamed about becoming a Little Brother and living the
gospel among men and women who had need of me and my
witness.

And who were these brothers and sisters of mine, in my
dream?

Whenever we think of "others" we have no choice but to
limit the picture in our mind, and narrow it down to some
particular group of people, depending on our experience, and
especially depending on our feelings.

One of us will think of the Chinese and say, "I'll devote
myself to the Chinese."

Someone else thinks of the poor of the Third World with
their starving babies, the peasants of Latin America, and decides, "I'll devote myself to them."

One of my fellow novices told me he wanted to sneak into
a country behind the Iron Curtain and devote himself to the
victims of atheistic propaganda.

Another one told me he would go to Hong Kong to work to
build a Christianity that would be equal to face the problems of
China when Hong Kong becomes part of China again.

Do you know what I wanted to do?

I was dreaming too and plans were taking shape in my heart and mind.

My dream was to go to the Alps and live with the Alpine rescue teams up on the Matterhorn and go with them to help people caught in storms.

Dreams don't happen by accident.

All my life I had been a mountain climber.

I'd been captain of an Alpine team, and the mountains were my passion.

I wanted to devote my passion to my fellow beings caught in the snow.

I wanted to be brother to Alpine guides and devote to their work, which is certainly not easy, my prayers and my service, as Jesus inspired me.

But I was only dreaming.

Do you know what happened to me in the middle of my dream?

I had to go on a four-hundred-mile hike through the Khaloua desert from El Abiodh.

I was not in very good condition and a male nurse, my friend, who took good care of me was concerned. "I'll give you some shots," he said. "You'll see, they'll keep you going."

"Fine," I said.

And with the best of intentions my friend stuck a needle in my thigh and injected me with a paralyzing poison. In less than twenty-four hours my leg was useless.

He had made a mistake.

He'd used the wrong vial.

It was stupid, but I would not say the nurse had been at fault except in the sense that he was impulsive and careless.

I didn't complain then, and I tried to keep cheerful if only to help the nurse whose fault it was not to go out of his mind. He was not as emotionally stable as I was.

I was paralyzed for life.

As soon as I felt a little better I started thinking things over. What about my dream now? What about the Alpine rescue team? Goodbye dream. Farewell any hope of ever climbing the Matterhorn. Suddenly I felt cheated.

How could I have been betrayed in this way?

I'd come to Africa to become a Little Brother.

I'd wanted to devote myself to people dying in snowstorms, I wanted to save them. Had I been wrong to want that?

What a perfectly miserable state of affairs!

How could the God I wanted to serve not reach out his hand when I needed him?

Why didn't he step in and stop such a simple, stupid mistake? Why didn't he help me? Why did he let. . . .

Sisters and brothers, let's stop for a moment. Let each of us think of our own suffering, our own trouble, our own paralysis, our own story. What am I doing here?

How did I get in this wheelchair?

What am I doing with this crutch?

How come I can't sleep at night?

How did I ever marry such a man, and then he abandons me to boot?

Why did that beam have to fall on me in the earthquake and crush my arm?

Why am I alone? What's wrong with just wanting to get married? And now there's no hope.

Why can't I draw just one easy breath of air?

Is someone else to blame for all this?

Or worse, is it because I'm so disordered inside?

And then, why does God, this so-called God, permit things like this? Why doesn't he step in in time?

Why did he just stand and watch while some idiot wretch beat me within an inch of my life and now I'll never be able to walk again?

Why didn't he make Herod die before he could carry out the slaughter in Bethlehem because Jesus was a thorn in his side?

Why didn't he step in and stop that storm blowing my hut away where I lived on the shore as a poor fisherman, as poor as Jesus himself?

Does this God exist or not?

Well, if he does, why doesn't he act, why doesn't he make an exception for me?

Here I came to serve him, and all he seems to do is mock me and let me turn into a cripple.

I thought it was a good idea to devote myself, as a mountaineer, to my fellow beings freezing to death in the snow!

And now what? What am I to do now?

Not join the Alpine rescue team, that's for sure!

So He's really switched things on me! Or could it be up to me to change plans?

Could be.

Thirty years have passed since then — thirty years since my dream went wrong.

Now here I am in front of you, and you have your dreams *too,* or have had them. And I can tell you something.

That mistaken injection that paralyzed my leg was not a stroke of bad luck. It was a grace.

Let's be precise. There's no point in pious platitudes.

It was bad luck, yes. It was a misfortune. But God turned it into a grace.

I had a useless leg. I could not climb. So I got a jeep and became a meteorologist.

Through no wish of my own, there I was where I belonged: in the desert.

Instead of trudging through the snow I trudged through the sand.

Instead of mountain passes I came to know caravan routes. Instead of chamois I saw gazelles.

Life suddenly appeared to me as it was, an immense personal exodus. Now I saw the desert as an extraordinary environment of silence and prayer.

My crippled leg helped me to "stand firm" (James 1:12).

I the runner — now stood firm.

I who'd always tried to do two things at once — now I stood firm. No doubt about it, it was a plus.

Deep down inside I began to understand that I hadn't been cheated. Misfortune had thrust me upon new paths.

Brothers and sisters before me with your misfortunes, I testify to you of one thing only.

Today, thirty years after the incident that paralyzed my leg, I don't say it wasn't a misfortune.

I only say that God was able to transform it into a grace. I have experienced in my flesh what Augustine says: "God permits evil, so as to transform it into a greater good."

God loves his children, and when he sees that someone or something has hurt them, what imagination he has — to transform the evil into good, inactivity into contemplation, the cry of pain into a prayer, grief into an act of love!

I know I'm only a child, telling you these things.

Smart people don't tell you. They're embarrassed.

Well, I'm going to come right out and tell you.

I've found no other answer to my pain.

And I know it by experience. You can be happy with a crippled leg.

Very happy.

In my experience the wounds of poverty and suffering produce a special, very precious, very sweet honey.

It's the honey of the Beatitudes proclaimed by Jesus in the Sermon on the Mount.

I have tasted this honey and have become convinced of the rationality of the gospel, of the reasons for so many mysterious things.

I have been convinced by experience.

I have come to believe in God through experience, and I always say: I believe in God because I know him.

And from suffering too.

There is still plenty of room for mystery. And it is right that this should be so, to educate us in humility, which is so important in our relationship with the Absolute that is God. But the thickest cloak that weighed on my misery and my blindness God has torn away, and the nakedness of my wounded flesh has helped me to recognize, out beyond the veil of mystery, the nakedness of God.

Only then, startled by joy, did I know the truth, that the encounter with the Eternal is possible. And that it is stupendous.

— Why O Lord?

2

The Wisdom of the Desert

NAZARETH

Charles de Foucauld, born in Strasbourg, September 15, 1858, was a nobleman. In his veins ran the blood of proud people accustomed to giving commands. He himself had attended the military academy of Saint-Cyr, had become an officer in the French army, and at the age of twenty-five had embarked on what was then a most dangerous undertaking — the exploration of Morocco.

Yet this man, soldier, adventurer — and apostate since his schooldays at Nancy — suddenly, in 1886, fell in love with Christ with the strength of a St. Francis.

Very rarely does one find a man more passionately dedicated to discovering the details of the life of Jesus. He searched in the Gospels for clues to Jesus' personality, character, and life, so that he might imitate the Lord's attitude, gestures, and innermost intentions; and in his loving search for faithful and living material for imitation, Charles de Foucauld was above all impressed by the fact that Jesus was poor and a workman. Astonishing! The Son of God — who, more than anyone else, was free to choose what he would — chose not only a mother and a people, but also a social position. And he wanted to be a wage earner.

That Jesus had *voluntarily* lost himself in an obscure Middle Eastern village; annihilated himself in the daily monotony of thirty years of rough, miserable work; separated himself from the society that "counts"; and died in total anonymity — all this confused the noble convert. (We must realize that the words "laborer," "worker," and "wage earner" have a quite different ring in the ears of a nobleman than they have in the average person's. Therefore it seemed to Charles de Foucauld that choosing to become a worker meant abasement, annihilation of oneself.)

Why hadn't Jesus become a scribe, he wondered? Why hadn't he wished to be born into one of those families destined for command, responsibility, social and political influence?

Not too long after de Foucauld began the passionate search for the intentions which had guided the Divine Master in the choice of his life, his whole life, he made the discovery that was to remain, basically, the ascetical guide of the life of this great Moroccan explorer and Saharan mystic: "Jesus has so diligently searched for the lowest place that it would be very difficult for anyone to tear it from him."

Nazareth was the lowest place: the place of the poor, the unknown, of those who didn't count, of the mass of workers, of men subjected to work's grim demands just for a scrap of bread.

But there is more. Jesus is the "Holy One of God." But the Holy One of God realized his sanctity not in an extraordinary life, but one impregnated with ordinary things: work, family, and social life, obscure human activities, simple things shared by all.

The perfection of God is cast in a material which people almost despise, which they don't consider worth searching for because of its simplicity, its lack of interest, because it is common to all men and women.

Once he had discovered the spiritual reality of Nazareth, Charles de Foucauld tried to imitate it as faithfully as possible.

He tried to found a community in a small home like the one at Nazareth; he tried to lose himself in the silence of an unknown village; he imitated Jesus by working manually, and he wanted his Little Brothers to be always searching for the last place, there where the poor are, where the climate is roughest, the wages the most meager, the toil hardest. Nazareth symbolized all this, and more.

The imitation of Nazareth is no small thing. When I think that a door, a wooden partition, was all that divided a holy family like that of Jesus from that of a neighbor, I am convinced of the immense interior richness of the gospel message. The same actions, if carried out under God's light, radically transformed the life of humanity, family, and society.

Joy or sadness, war or peace, love or hate, purity or impurity, charity or greed, all are tremendous realities that are the hinges of a person's interior life. Everyday things, relationships with our fellow humans, daily work, love of our family — all these may breed saints.

Jesus at Nazareth taught us to live every hour of the day as saints. Every hour of the day is useful and may lead to divine inspiration, the will of the Father, the prayer of contemplation — holiness. Every hour of the day is holy. What matters is to live it as Jesus taught us.

And for this one does not have to shut oneself in a monastery or fix strange and inhumane regimes for one's life. It is enough to accept the realities of life. Work is one of these realities; motherhood, the rearing of children, family life with all its obligations are others.

These realities must be sanctified; we must not think that a person is holy just because he has made vows. One with this outlook thinks of the hour of spiritual reading or prayer as the only time for the spiritual life and ignores the longer time dedicated to work and everyday living. The result is at best an anemic and unreliable religious personality.

The whole person must be transformed by the gospel message. Nothing one does can be indifferent. All one's actions must be determined by the gospel.

Nazareth is the life of a human being, of a family, fully engaged in human activity.

Few have summed up the sanctity of common things so well as did Gandhi in his writings:

> If when we plunge our hand into a bowl of water,
> Or stir up the fire with the bellows
> Or tabulate interminable columns of figures on our
>   book-keeping table,
> Or, burnt by the sun, we are plunged in the mud of
>   the rice-field,
> Or standing by the smelter's furnace
> We do not fulfill the same religious life as if in prayer
>   in a monastery, the world will never be saved.

But there is another aspect of Nazareth that is important above all for those who think it is impossible to carry out the gospel message without tools, means, or money.

Jesus was himself the carrier of the message; he was at the same time the Supreme Intelligence, capable of devising the best way of making himself understood, and of carrying out the divine plans.

Well, what did he do? He did not open hospitals or found orphanages. He became flesh, lived among people, and embodied the gospel message in its entirety, *Coepit facere*. He began to act.

He lived his message before he *spoke* of it. He preached it by his life before explaining it in words. This was Jesus' method and we too easily forget it.

In many cases catechesis is reduced to words rather than to "life," to discussions rather than to the pursuit of Christian living.

And here, perhaps, is the reason for the poor results, and still more, the reason for so much of the apathy and indifference among Christians today. Teaching is ineffective because it is not life-centered; there is no life because there is no example; there is no example because empty words have taken the place of faith and charity.

"I want to preach the gospel with my life," Charles de Foucauld often said. He was convinced that the most effective method of preaching the gospel was to live it. Especially today, people no longer want to listen to sermons. They want to see the gospel in action.

Nazareth is the long period of separation, prayer, and sacrifice. It is a time of silence, of intimate life with God; the time of long solitude, purification, understanding humanity, and knowing the value of detachment: the things that matter to a Christian.

From Nazareth we will learn how to live the gospel....

— *Letters from the Desert*

•

I was living in the Hoggar in a fraternity of the Little Brothers of Charles de Foucauld, and I was earning my bread by working as a meteorologist in the region of Tit, Tazrouk, and In Amguel. I enjoyed the work not only because it provided me with food but because it gave me the opportunity to live in the place of my choice, namely, the desert, and to unite my daily task with its huge silences and the possibility of prolonged prayer.

Before long I got to know the Tuaregs who lived in tents, the Aratini who cultivated the oases, the Arabs who came from the north, and the Mozabites who specialized in commerce.

I was particularly fond of the Tuaregs whose tents were pitched along the *guelta,* a rocky basin where water surfaces, and on the uplands; and as I journeyed I often stayed with them in the evenings after my work.

It was during an encounter of this kind that I became aware of an interesting fact.

Quite by chance I discovered that a girl in the camp where I was staying was betrothed to a boy in another camp, but she hadn't yet gone to live with him because he was too young. I could not help linking this piece of information with that passage in the Gospel where it says that the Virgin Mary was betrothed to Joseph but they had not yet come together (Matt. 1:18).

Two years later I went back to that camp and, looking for a topic for conversation, asked if the marriage had yet taken place. There was a look of embarrassment on my interlocutor's face followed by an awkward silence.

So I did not pursue the subject. But later that evening, when I went to draw water at the *guelta* about a hundred yards from the camp, I fell in with one of the chief's servants and asked him the meaning of the awkward silence.

The servant looked cautiously around; then, because he trusted me as being a *marabout,* * he made a sign that I knew well — he passed his hand under his chin in a gesture characteristic of the Arabs when they want to convey that someone has had his or her throat cut.

The reason?

Before the wedding it was discovered that the girl was pregnant and the honor of the betrayed family required this sacrifice.

A shiver went down my spine to think that the girl had been killed because she had not been faithful to her future husband.

That evening at compline, beneath the Sahara sky, I read Matthew's account of the conception of Jesus. I had to light a candle because it was a dark, moonless night. I read: "When his mother Mary had been betrothed to Joseph, before they came together she was found to be with child of the Holy Spirit; and her husband Joseph, being a just man and unwilling to put her to shame, resolved to send her away quietly" (Matt. 1:18–19).

So Joseph had not denounced her, nor had her father, Joachim, ... killed her as the law decreed — "Moses commanded us to stone such" (John 8:4).

---

*A man of God.

I remember vividly how it was on that evening. I felt that Mary was very close, squatting on the sand, small, weak, defenseless, with her large belly, unable to lean forward, silent.

I put out the candle.

But I saw shining eyes all around me, eyes like jackals' eyes when they are waiting for little lambs.

They were the eyes of the inhabitants of Nazareth spying on the girl-mother and asking her with all the force of incredulity that men, and still more women, are capable of: "What have you done to have that child, you dissolute wretch, you slut!"

What a night!

What could I answer?

That God is the baby's father?

Who would believe me?

I said nothing.

God knows.

God provides.

Poor gentle Mary, poor little girl-mother. What a bad start to your life!

How are you going to face so many enemies, and who will believe you?

After I had been told that the girl-mother in the Tuareg encampment had been killed because she was caught in adultery, my relations with Mary of Nazareth became much closer.

It was as if she suddenly became my sister. I was not used to seeing her so human, so frail, so near to me. The liturgy had fostered a supernatural relationship, yes, but it had stifled Mary's voice as a woman, a creature, a sister, a teacher — a voice that just beside me could say so much more to me.

Yes, I must humbly admit it. It was not until I saw that silent tragedy of the Tuareg encampment in the light of Luke's Gospel that I fully understood Mary's courage in accepting what the angel told her about God's plans for her. She had to accept the role of a girl-mother.

And who was going to believe her? If a young girl had come to my home in Piedmont and said, "But I assure you, this baby I'm carrying is the son of the Most High," no one would have believed her.

In my home my father would certainly have given her a slap in the face, and that was Piedmont. Further south she would have been told to get out: "We don't want to see you ever again; you've disgraced the family."

In an Arab or Scythian or Jewish family in past times, blood would have flowed.

Mary had the courage to trust in the God of the impossible and to leave the solution of her problems to him. Hers was pure faith. We must not forget that the Bible was written precisely in that region between the desert and the steppe where there are wandering caravans, where sheep and asses graze, where men know how to question the sky because it is their only hope of life.

And I was there too. When at night I set up camp at the side of the track and lit the fire to bake the bread and boil the tea, Mary came and joined me. I had only to bring out my rosary, which I myself had made (its beads were cut from wood collected in Issakarassem) and which I always carried in my pocket, to feel Mary's presence beside the fire. The desert is a huge church with the starry sky as the vault and the fine hot sand as the mat on which to sit and pray.

What pleasure to forget the notion of time and space and live the communion of saints as a tender reality.

It was for this that I came to the desert. I longed to break the barrier between the visible and the invisible, between the sky and the earth, and in faith I often succeeded.

What peace to penetrate beyond the world of things! To live as if the gospel was being written now, being lived now.

To see the symbol of God as manifested in things fading away and revealing his invisible presence, his divine reality.

To be able to speak with the saints....

— Blessed Are You Who Believed

THE FRIENDLY NIGHT

When I first came to the Sahara I was afraid of the night.

For some, night means more work, for others dissipation, for still others insomnia, boredom.

For me now it's quite different. Night is first of all rest, real rest. At sunset a great serenity sets in, as though nature were obeying a sudden sign from God.

The wind which has howled all day ceases, the heat dies down, the atmosphere becomes clear and limpid, and great peace spreads everywhere, as though humanity and the elements wanted to refresh themselves after the great battle with the day and its sun.

Yes, the night here is different. It has not lost its purity, its mystery. It has remained as God made it, his creation, bringer of good and life. With your work finished and the caravan halted, you stretch out on the sand with a blanket under your head and breathe in the gentle breeze which has replaced the dry, fiery daytime wind.

Then you leave the camp and go down to the dunes for prayer. Time passes undisturbed. No obligations harass you, no noise disturbs you, no worry awaits you: time is all yours. So you satiate yourself with prayer and silence, while the stars light up in the sky.

Those who have never seen them cannot believe what the stars are like in the desert; the complete absence of artificial light, the vastness of the horizon only seem to increase their number and brightness. It is certainly an unforgettable experience. Only the campfire with the tea water boiling on top and the bread for supper baking underneath, glows with a mellow light against the sparkling heaven.

The first nights spent here made me send off for books on astronomy and maps of the sky; and for months afterward I spent my free time learning a little of what was passing over my head up there in the Universe.

It was all good material for my prayer of adoration. Kneeling on the sand I sank my eyes for hours and hours in those wonders, writing down my discoveries in an exercise book like a child.

I understood, for example, that finding one's way in the desert is much easier by night than by day, that the points of reference are numerous and certain. In the years that I spent in the open desert I never once got lost, thanks to the stars.

Many times, when searching for a Tuareg camp or a lost weather station, I lost my way because the sun was too high in the sky. But I waited for night and found the road again, guided by the stars.

The Saharan night is not only a wonderful time for repose; it also provides a restful dwelling place for the soul. After the day — with all that light — the soul closes up like a house without windows to have their shutters unhinged by the wind or burnt by the sun.

I shall never forget the nights under the Saharan stars. I felt as if I were wrapped around by the blanket of the friendly night, a blanket embroidered with stars.

Yes, a friendly night, a benevolent darkness with restful shadows. In them the movement of my soul is not hindered. On the contrary, it can spread out, be fulfilled, grow, and be joyful.

I feel at home, safe, fearless, desirous only of staying like this for hours; my only worry that of the shortness of the night so avid am I to read within and outside myself the symbols of divine language.

The friendly night is an image of faith, that gift of God defined, "The guarantee of the blessings we hope for and proof of the existence of the realities that at present remain unseen" (Heb. 11:1).

I have never found a better metaphor for my relationship with the Eternal: a point lost in infinite space, wrapped round by the night under the subdued light of the stars.

I am this point lost in space: the darkness, like an irreplaceable friend, is faith. The stars, God's witness.

When my faith was weak, all this would have seemed incomprehensible to me. I was afraid as a child is of the night. But now I have conquered it, and it is mine. I experience joy in night, navigating upon it as upon the sea. The night is no longer my enemy, nor does it make me afraid. On the contrary, its darkness and divine transcendence are a source of delight.

Sometimes I even close my eyes to see more darkness. I know the stars are there in their place, as a witness to me of heaven. And I can see why darkness is so necessary.

The darkness is necessary, the darkness of faith is necessary, for God's light is too great. It wounds.

I understand more and more that faith is not a mysterious and cruel trick of a God who hides himself without telling me why, but a necessary veil. My discovery of him takes place gradually, respecting the growth of divine life in me.

"No one may see God and live," says the Scripture, in the sense that to see him face to face is possible only for those who have passed beyond death.

On earth such is the light, the infinity of the mystery, and the inadequacy of human nature, that I must penetrate it little by little. First through symbols, then through experience, and finally in the contemplation which I can achieve on this earth if I remain faithful to God's love.

But it will be only a beginning, getting the eyes of my soul accustomed to so much light: the process will go on endlessly and the mystery will remain as long as we are dominated by God's infinity.

What is our life on earth, if not discovering, becoming conscious of, penetrating, contemplating, accepting, loving this mystery of God's, the unique reality that surrounds us, and in which we are immersed like meteorites in space? "In God we live and move and have our being" (Acts 17:28).

There aren't many mysteries, but there is one upon which everything depends, and it is so immense that it fills the whole space.

Human discoveries do not help us to penetrate this mystery. Future millennia will illuminate no further what Isaiah said and what God himself declared to Moses before the burning bush, "I am who I am" (Exod. 3:4).

Perhaps the sky was less dark for Abraham and those with the tents than for modern men and women; perhaps faith was simpler for medieval poets than present-day technicians. But the situation is the same, and the nature of our relationship with God does not change.

The more one grows in maturity, the more one is required to have faith, devoid of sentiment. But the road will remain the same until the last has been born on this earth.

Mary and Joseph, you it is who are masters of faith, perfect examples to inspire us, correct our course, and support our weakness.

Just as you were beside Jesus, you are still beside us to accompany us to eternal life, to teach us to be small and poor in our work, humble and hidden in life, courageous in trial, faithful in prayer, ardent in love.

And when the hour of our death comes and dawn rises over our friendly night, our eyes, as they scan the sky, may pick out the same star that was in your sky when Jesus came upon the earth.   — *Letters from the Desert*

BRIDGING THE GAP

At Tazrouk in the Hoggar the Little Brothers had a fraternity among the ex-slaves of the Tuareg, poor families who lived by cultivating a bit of grain and a few vegetables along the *oued*.

The *oued* of Tazrouk was a haven of peace, and the brothers too had their garden, where they worked the soil.

But what a labor it was to draw something forth from that sand! If there was not a drought, the locusts descended, and if one escaped the locusts there were caterpillars instead. And what is more, rabbits used to come in from round about and make short work of the little bit of green that had been acquired as the result of so much effort.

By way of self-defense, therefore, one was compelled to set traps, and these became the source of a bit of meat which was generally not too bad — as long as it was not fox or jackal.

One evening a flight of storks appeared in the sky above Tazrouk, bound for the north: it was spring at the time.

Descending in wide circles, the birds came to pass the night on the *oued*. In her efforts to find somewhere to alight, a beautiful female stork put her foot right into one of the traps. All that night she lost blood, and when the dawn came, and her companions realized what was happening, it was too late. All attempts to save the poor bird were useless: she died that same day and we buried her at the edge of the *oued*. But then began the drama that involved each of us intimately. The flight of storks set out once more for the north, but the partner of the dead stork stayed behind at the *oued*. That evening we saw the wretched bird come down near the garden, in the same place that his partner had been trapped, and fly round and round, crying and showing by obvious signs that he was looking for something. This went on until sunset. The same scene was repeated the next day. The flight of storks had possibly reached the Mediterranean by now, and yet this lone bird was still there, searching for his companion. He stayed for the entire year. Each day he would go off in search of food, and at sunset we would see his outline against the sky over the garden, as he came down in the usual place, crying, searching and finally going to sleep in the sand where, perhaps, he could still detect the smell of his partner's blood.

The brothers became accustomed to the stork, as he did to them. He would fly into the garden and come over to take whatever morsel of meat or moistened bread the brothers offered him.

It was moving to see how sensitive this creature was to the love and attention of the brothers, who, feeling themselves to be somehow responsible for his bereavement, redoubled their attentions.

I remember the look in his eyes, his habit of cocking his head on one side, the regular movement of his beak, and the way he had of staring at me, as if he were trying to catch hold of me and escape from his solitude.

I for my part tried to understand him, but I remained myself, and he remained a stork. I remained imprisoned within my limitations as he did within his — limitations fixed for us by nature.

There was no possibility of communication.

And yet this migrant had done, and knew how to do, extraordinary things, things that I myself would have been incapable of doing.

He had left the hot countries — Mali, perhaps, or Niger — and he had traveled hundreds of miles with neither compass nor radar; he was capable of continuing his journey without a map, until finally he came back to the same roof-top, the same chimney-pot as last year and there build his nest. And yet . . . for all his skill as a long distance navigator, he would not have known how to read my language or interpret the intonation of my voice.

The following spring another flight of storks reached the *oued* of Tazrouk. This time our friend joined it, and set out once more for the north.

I have often thought about that bird as I searched for a comparison or tried to explain the gulf that exists between the nature of animals and the nature of human beings. Comparisons are of limited value, but they can help us in our weakness.

There is also an unbridgeable gulf between the nature of God and the nature of human beings — there is the fact of transcendence.

And herein lies the mystery kept hidden, as St. Paul says, through many centuries, and revealed to us in the fullness of time.

God, in his love, decided to bridge the gulf, making it possible for a human being to become in every respect his son.

It is as if, with a power I do not in fact possess, I had somehow enabled the stork to achieve the impossible and become my child, and therefore capable of understanding me, of communicating with me, of living my life, sharing my intelligence, my love, my will. . . .

Born of God, I who was born of a man and a woman whom I learned, from my earliest years, to call mother and father! What a profound mystery! Nicodemus was right to be perplexed by Jesus' statements.

How can one bridge the unbridgeable?

Given the fact that God offers us such a priceless gift, how are we to make it a reality for ourselves? How can we turn it into something authentic, living, true?

If God was prompted by love to make so radical an offering, how could human beings respond adequately? How could we freely make it our own?

Who would show us the Father's house, familiarize us with his language, his customs, his will?

Who, in short, would "reveal" God to us?

Enable us to approach the heart of his inexpressible knowledge?

Make it possible for us to make the transition to another nature which spelled complete darkness in terms of our understanding, our language?

Who would overcome the problem of God's otherness, bridge the gulf that separates creature from creator, human from God?

Who would make it clear to me what I ought to do?

Who would pass on to me his own life, his personal knowledge?...In order to achieve the impossible, the God of the impossible took the first step himself. What human beings were unable to do for ourselves God has done by stooping down toward us. To enable us to take our place in the family of God, God entered the human family. With the Incarnation for the first time the unbridgeable was bridged from above to below. Something that had never happened before — that one from above should come down to us — happened in Jesus.

The invisible became visible, the intangible became tangible in Christ. History has been shocked into new life since Jesus came to play a part in it: the cosmos has become a sacred offering since the Word took flesh from a woman living within the cosmos.

God has become human, the Word has become a child, Immensity has accepted limitations.

The infinite has become finite.

The unknowable has made himself known.

Omnipotence became a child.

The immutable accepted suffering.

The perfect one took on the burden of sin.

Life was attained through death.

Love was expressed as resurrection.

Jesus became our brother....

— *In Search of the Beyond*

SHEPHERDS WITH THEIR FLOCKS

During advent I found myself in the pale hot hills of Béni-Abbès, that fantastic oasis in the Sahara.

I wanted to prepare myself for Christmas in solitude, and the place I had chosen was Ouarourout, where water was abundant and a small natural cave could serve as a chapel.

I set out after the feast of the Immaculate Conception (December 8) in wonderful weather and with a great longing to be alone.

But the weather soon changed and the desert became cold and gray due to the high mist that covered the sun.

And even my solitude was not what I expected, for soon I was discovered by Ali, son of Mohamed Assani. Ali was a good friend who brought his eleven sheep to graze round about and was thirsting for company and conversation. He assured me that he couldn't find better or richer pastures for his flock than near the well of Ouarourout.

He kept his distance, of course, because he knew that when I was praying he had to keep away and not disturb me.

But the well was common property so naturally he took the opportunity of coming near when I went to draw water, and then he profited by the occasion to invite me to tea — having taken all the necessaries from my tent.

Ali made tea very well, and he loved drinking it with me; he also liked my bread, which I baked under the ashes.

Then off he went to the pastures and for the whole day contented himself with keeping his eye on me from a distance while he searched the sand for little fossils and archeological remains such as tips of arrows from the stone age, which he could then come and sell to me.

The weather grew worse and I had to reinforce my tent ropes against the windstorm which would surely follow. Windstorms in the desert are appalling, developing as they do into sandstorms, and anyone who has been in the desert knows what a sandstorm is like.

To describe the sort of thing that can happen, suffice it to say that even at midday you have to switch on the headlights of the van if you want to see the track, and the windows and the paintwork are nearly worn away by the violence of the sand.

My one refuge was my cave, and, when the storm came, there I decided to stay night and day so as not to interrupt my retreat.

As for Ali, I had not seen him for a day or two so I told myself that he must have foreseen the storm and prudently returned to the fold and his father's tent situated about eight miles from Ouarourout, at the intersection with the road to Bechar.

Not a bit of it!

There I was praying in my cave when he came rushing in, crook in hand and wild with worry.

"Come quickly, Brother Carlo, come and help me. My sheep are lost, they're dying in the sand."

I dashed to the van and together we plunged into the desert, a desert furious with blinding wind and sand.

It wasn't easy to find the sheep in that inferno. They were frightened and enfeebled and wandering helplessly in the gusts of sand and rain which had now started to fall.

I have never seen anything like it. Once again I realized how narrow is the line between life and death in the desert.

While I was at the steering wheel and trying not to get lost, Ali was pouncing on his sheep and piling them one by one into the van — they were weak with exhaustion and numb with fear.

Somehow we managed to get them into my cave, the only possible refuge from the breathtaking hurricane. So my little cave was full of wooliness, of bleating, and of the acrid smell of sheep.

I was reminded of the cave at Bethlehem, and I tried to get warm by snuggling up against the largest sheep — they were as drenched as I was and shivering in the evening dusk.

I took the Eucharist from the tabernacle and hung the pyx round my neck under my cloak.

Naturally we did not manage to light the fire for supper, so we had to be satisfied with eating bread and a tin of sardines.

But Ali liked the sardines.

For myself, I wanted to pray, and I soon realized that things hadn't gone too badly for me in the turmoil of the storm.

Wasn't I living through a very special night?

It was near to Christmas.

I was in a cave with a shepherd.

I was cold.

There were sheep and the stench of dung.

Nothing was missing.

The Eucharist that I had hung round my neck made me think of Jesus present there under the sign of bread, so like the sign of Bethlehem, the land of bread.

The night advanced. Outside the storm continued to rage over the desert.

Now all was silence in the cave.

The sheep filled up the available space.

Ali slept curled in his cloak with his head resting on the back of a sheep and with two lambs at his feet.

Meanwhile I prayed, reciting Luke's Gospel from memory:

"And while they were there, the time came for her to be delivered. And she gave birth to her first-born son and wrapped him in swaddling cloths, and laid him in a manger, because there was no place for them in the inn" (Luke 2:6). Then I was silent and waited.

Mary became my prayer and I felt her to be very, very close to me. Jesus was in the Eucharist just there under my cloak.

All my faith, all my hope, all my love were united in one point.

I had no need to meditate; I only had to contemplate in silence. The whole night was at my disposal and dawn was still far off. *— Blessed Are You Who Believed*

CONTEMPLATION IN THE STREETS

Charles de Foucauld said one day: "If the contemplative life were possible only behind convent walls or in the silence of the desert we would, in fairness, give a little convent to every mother of a family, and a track of desert to every person working hard in a bustling city to earn his living."

The vision of the reality in which the majority of the poor live determined the central crisis of his life; the crisis which was to carry him far from his first understanding of the religious life.

As you may know, Charles de Foucauld was a Trappist and had chosen the poorest Trappist monastery in existence, that of Akbes in Syria. One day his superior sent him to watch by the corpse of a Christian Arab who had died in a poor house.

When Brother Charles was in the dead man's hovel he saw real poverty around him: hungry children and a weak, defenseless widow without assurance of the next day's bread. It was this spiritual crisis that was to make him leave La Trappe and go in search of a religious life very different from the earlier one.

"We, who have chosen the imitation of Jesus and Jesus Crucified, are very far from the trials, the pains, the insecurity and the poverty to which these people are subjected.

"I no longer want a monastery that is too secure. I want a small monastery, like the house of a poor workman who is not sure if tomorrow he will find work and bread, who with all his being shares the suffering of the world.

"Oh, Jesus, a monastery like your house at Nazareth, in which to live hidden as you did when you came among us."

When he came out of La Trappe, Foucauld founded his first fraternity at Béni-Abbès in the Sahara; later he built his hermitage at Tamanrasset, where he died, murdered by the Tuareg.

The fraternity was to resemble the house of Nazareth, a house just like one of the many houses one sees along the many streets of the world.

Had he renounced contemplation then? Had his fervid spirit of prayer weakened? No, he had taken a step forward. He had decided to live the contemplative life along the streets, in a situation similar to that of any ordinary man.

That step is much harder!

It is a step that God wants us to make.

The life of Charles de Foucauld opens up a new understanding of the spiritual life in which many will force themselves to make the fusion between contemplation and action — really living and obeying the first commandment of the Lord, "Love God above all things and your neighbor as yourself."

"Contemplation in the streets." This is tomorrow's task not only for the Little Brothers, but for all the poor.

Let us begin to analyze this element of "desert" that must be present, especially today, in the carrying out of such a demanding program.

When one speaks of the soul's desert, and says that the desert must be present in your life, you must not think only of the Sahara or the desert of Judea, or into the High Valley of the Nile.

Certainly it is not everyone who can have the advantage of being able to carry out in practice this detachment from daily life. The Lord conducted me into the real desert because I was so thick-skinned. For *me*, it was necessary. But all that sand was not enough to erase the dirt from my soul; even the fire was not enough to remove the rust from Ezekiel's pot.

But the same way is not for everybody. And if you cannot go into the desert, you must nonetheless "make some desert" in your life. Every now and then leaving others and looking for solitude to restore, in prolonged silence and prayer, the stuff of your soul. This is the meaning of "desert" in your spiritual life.

One hour a day, one day a month, eight days a year, for longer if necessary, you must leave everything and everybody and retire, alone with God. If you don't look for this solitude, if you don't love it, you won't achieve real contemplative prayer. If you are able to do so but nevertheless do not withdraw in order to enjoy intimacy with God, the fundamental element of the relationship with the All-Powerful is lacking: love. And without love no revelation is possible.

But the desert is not the final stopping place. It is a stage on the journey. Because, as I told you, our vocation is contemplation in the streets.

For me, this is quite costly. The desire to continue living here in the Sahara forever is so strong that I am already suffering in anticipation of the order that will certainly come from my superiors: "Brother Charles, leave for Marseilles, leave for Morocco, leave for Venezuela, leave for Detroit.

"You must go back among men and women, mix with them, live your intimacy with God in the noise of their cities. It will be difficult but you must do it. And for this the grace of God will not fail you.

"Every morning, after Mass and meditation, you will make your way to work in a store or shipyard. And when you get back in the evening, tired, like all poor men and women forced to earn their living, you will enter the little chapel of the brotherhood and remain for a long time in adoration, bringing to your prayer all that world of suffering, of darkness, and often of sin, in the midst of which you have lived for eight hours, taking your share of pain and toil."

Contemplation in the streets. A good phrase, but very demanding. Certainly it would be easier and more pleasant to stay here in the desert. But God doesn't seem to want that.

The voice of the Church makes itself heard more and more. It points out to Christians the reality of the mystical body and the People of God.

It calls us to the life of love. It invites everybody to a life of action which, couched in contemplation, is a witness and presence among human beings.

Convent walls are becoming thinner and the ceilings ever lower. The laity are becoming conscious of their mission and are searching for a genuine spirituality. It is truly the dawn of a new world to which it would not seem unworthy to give as an aim "contemplation in the streets" and to offer the means of achieving it....   — *Letters from the Desert*

•

The desert...the desert...the desert!

I only have to say this word to feel my whole being rise up and move forward even while physically it remains where it is.

It signifies the awareness that it is God who saves, that without God I am "in the shadow of death" and that to emerge from the darkness I must put myself on the path that God will show me.

It is the path of Exodus, it is the march of the People of God from the slavery of idols to the freedom of the Promised Land, to the joy and brightness of the kingdom.

And this, by crossing the desert.

But the word "desert" is much more than a geographical expression that suggests to our minds a derelict, parched, and arid expanse of land with no one in it.

The word "desert" — for the person who lets him or herself be taken up by the Spirit — expresses the search for God in silence. It is a "suspension bridge" thrown by the soul in love with God over the dark abyss of its own spirit, over the strange deep crevasses of temptation, over the unfathomable precipices of its own fears which form an obstacle to the progress toward God.

"Yes, such a desert is holy and is a prayer beyond all prayer. It leads to the continuous presence of God and to the heights of contemplation where the soul, at peace at last, lives by the will of him whom it loves totally, absolutely, and endlessly" (Catherine de Hueck Doherty).

I told you that the word "desert" means much more than a mere geographical place.

The Russians, who understand these things and are our masters in these matters, call it *poustinia*.

Poustinia may mean a geographical desert, but at the same time it may mean the place to which the Desert Fathers withdrew. It may mean hermitage, a quiet place to which people withdraw so as to find God in silence and prayer, a place where — as a Russian mystic living in America puts it — "we can raise the arms of prayer and penance toward God in expiation, intercession, and reparation for our own sins and the sins of our brothers and sisters. The desert is the place where we gather courage, where we pronounce words of truth remembering that God is truth. The desert is the place where we purify ourselves and prepare ourselves to act as if touched by the burning coal that was placed by the angel on the lips of the Prophet."

The point is — and this is the characteristic that I want to underline — the point is that *poustinia* for the Russians, as well as for ourselves who are in the same spiritual line of mystical experience, accompanies us wherever we go and does not abandon us because we are not in the desert.

In other words: if someone cannot go to the desert, then the desert can come to him or her.

That is why we talk about "making a desert in the city."

Make yourself a little *poustinia* in your house, in your garden, in your attic. Do not dissociate the concept of desert from the places where men and women live their lives. Try both in your thoughts and in your lives to put this glorious phrase into practice: "the desert in the heart of the city."

Père de Foucauld, one of the most tireless seekers after modern spirituality, set up his hermitage at Béni-Abbès in a context where he could be open to God and at the same time open to human beings.

And when he decided to build a wall around it, he stopped when the wall was two feet high. This was so that the people living in the neighboring oases could easily climb over it when they wanted to visit him.

The wall remained, however, as a "sign" of his monastic isolation. The desert occupied his life more profoundly.

Yes, we must create a desert in the heart of crowded places.

It is a practical way of helping people now.

It is the pressing problem. It is constantly spoken of.

It is in the air.... 　　　　　　　　　*— The Desert in the City*

UNDER THE GREAT ROCK

The track, white in the sun, unwound ahead of me in a vague outline. The furrows in the sand made by the wheels of the great oil trucks forced me to keep alert every second, if I was to keep the jeep on the move.

The sun was high in the sky, and I felt tired. Only the wind blowing on the hood of the car allowed the jeep to continue, although the temperature was like hell-fire and the water was boiling in the radiator. Every now and then I fixed my gaze on the horizon. I knew that in the area there were great blocks of granite embedded in the sand: they provided highly desirable sources of shade under which to pitch camp and wait the evening before proceeding with the journey.

In fact, toward midday, I found what I was looking for. Great rocks appeared on the left of the track. I approached, in the hope that I would find a little shade. I was not disappointed. On the north wall of the thirty-foot-high slab of stone, a knife of shade was thrown on to the red sand. I pulled the jeep against the wind to cool the engine and unloaded the *ghess,* the necessary equipment for pitching camp: a bag of food, two blankets, and a tripod for the fire....

I spread out the mat. In the desert it is everything: chapel, dining room, bedroom, drawing-room. It was the hour of Sext. I sat down, took out my breviary, and recited a few Psalms, but I had to force myself because I was so tired. Warm sultry air was coming from the south, and my head ached. I got up. I calculated how much water I had to last me until I reached the well of Tit, and decided to sacrifice a little. From the goatskin gourd I drew a basinful of two pints and poured it on my head. The water soaked into my turban, ran down my neck and on to my clothes. The wind did the rest. From 115 degrees the temperature descended in a few minutes to 80 degrees. With that sense of refreshment I stretched out on the sand to sleep; in the desert you take your siesta before your meal.

In order to lie more comfortably I looked for a blanket to put under my head. I had two. One remained by my side unused, and as I looked at it I could not feel at ease.

But to understand you must hear my story.

The evening before I had passed through Irafog, a small village of Negroes, ex-slaves of the Tuareg. As usual when one reaches a village the people ran out to crowd round the jeep, either from curiosity or to obtain the various things that desert travelers bring with them: they may bring a little tea, distribute medicines, or hand over letters.

That evening I had seen old Kada trembling with cold. It seems strange to speak of cold in the desert, but it is so; in fact the Sahara is often called "a cold country where it is very hot in the sun." The sun had gone down, and Kada was shivering. I had the idea of giving him one of the blankets I had with me, an essential part of my *ghess;* but I put the thought out of my mind. I thought of the night, and I knew that I, too, would shiver. The little charity that was in me made me think again, though reasoning that my skin wasn't worth more than his and that I had best give him one of the blankets. Even if I shivered a little that was the least a Little Brother could do.

When I left the village the blankets were still on the jeep; and now they were giving me a bad conscience.

I tried to get to sleep with my feet resting on the great rock, but I couldn't manage it. I remembered that a month ago a Tuareg in the middle of his siesta had been crushed by a falling slab. I got up to make sure how stable the boulder was; I saw that it was a little off-balance, but not enough to be dangerous.

I lay down again on the sand. If I were to tell you what I dreamed of you would find it strange. The funny thing is that I dreamed that I was asleep under the great boulder and that at a given moment — it didn't seem to be a dream at all: I saw the rock moving, and I felt the boulder fall on top of me. What a nightmare! I felt my bones grating and I found myself dead. No, alive, but with my body crushed under the stone. I was amazed that not a bone hurt; but I could not move. I opened my eyes and saw Kada shivering in front of me at Irafog. I didn't hesitate for a minute to give him the blanket, especially as it was lying unused behind me, a yard away. I tried to stretch out my hand to offer it to him; but the stone made even the smallest movement impossible. I understood what purgatory was and that the suffering of the soul was "no longer to have the possibility of doing what before one could and should have done." Who knows for how many years afterward I would be haunted by seeing that blanket near me as a witness to my selfishness and to the fact that I was too immature to enter the kingdom of love.

I tried to think of how long I was to remain under the rock. The reply was given me by the catechism: "Until you are capable of an act of perfect love." At that moment I felt quite incapable.

The perfect act of love is Jesus going up to Calvary to die for us all. As a member of his Mystical Body I was being asked to show if I was close enough to that perfect love to follow my master to Calvary for the salvation of my brothers and sisters. The presence of the blanket denied to Kada the evening before told me that I had still a long way to go. If I were capable of passing by a brother who was shivering with cold, how should I be capable of dying for him in imitation of Jesus, who died for us all? In this way I understood that I was lost, and that if somebody had not come to my aid, I should have lain there, eon after eon, without being able to move.

I looked away and realized that all those great rocks in the desert were nothing more than the tombs of other men. They too, judged according to their ability to love and found cold, were there to await him who once said, "I shall raise you up on the last day...."

Even now I could not tell you if the episode of the great rock were a dream, let alone what kind of dream. Its influence upon me has been so strong, my attitude toward things so changed by it, that I have never been able to describe it as what we commonly have in mind when we say upon waking, "I have had a dream."

No, for me that tract of desert between Tit and Silet is still the place of my purgatory, where I was forced to meditate seriously about the ways of God and where I shall probably ask to go after death to continue my expiation, if in life I have not been capable of performing an act of perfect love....

What's the use of saying the Divine Office well, of sharing the Eucharist, if one is not impelled by love?

What's the use of giving up everything and coming here to the desert and the heat, if only to resist love?

What's the good of defending the truth, fighting over dogmas with the theologians, getting shocked at those who haven't the same faith, and then living purgatory for geological epochs?

"You will be judged according to your ability to love," says the great stone under which I spent my purgatory waiting for perfect love to grow within myself, that which Jesus brought to earth for me, and gave me at the price of his blood, shot through with the great cry of hope, "I shall raise you up on the last day" (John 6:40).

May that day be not far off.   — Letters from the Desert

3

God Is Love

YOU LIVING IN ME, AND I LIVING IN YOU

When I was a boy I looked for God by directing my gaze toward the light coming from on high.

As a young lad I looked for God in my brothers and sisters around me.

When I grew up I sought God along desert tracks.

Now I have come to the end of the road; I have only to close my eyes and there God is, within me.

If I see light I see God in the light, and if I see darkness I feel God in the darkness. But always within me.

I no longer even feel the need to search for God, or to kneel down to pray, or to think or speak in order to communicate with God.

I only need to think of my human state — and there, in faith, I see God in the midst.

You living in me and I living in you, I say with John. And John it is, the great gospel mystic, who records yet another of Jesus' sayings, surely the most concise of all the syntheses of contemplation and action, of heaven and earth, of doing and being: "Live on in my love" (see John 15:9).

Live on ... Live on. ...

When anyone asks me, especially after I have come back from the desert, "Brother Carlo, do you believe in God?" I answer: "Yes, I tell you in the Holy Spirit, I do believe."

And if my questioner's curiosity is aroused, to the point of inquiring further: "What evidence do you bring forward for asserting so great a truth?" I say, to conclude the conversation, "Only this: I believe in God because I know him."

I experience God's presence in me twenty-four hours out of twenty-four. I know and love his word without ever questioning it. I am aware of God's tastes and preferences, his way of speaking, and, especially, his will.

But here precisely, as regards knowing his will, is where things suddenly get difficult.

When I think that God's will is Christ himself, and Christ's way of living and dying for love, I see God withdraw infinitely far from me. God turns out to be far, far away. So far away, that he is inaccessible.

How could I ever live as Jesus lived?

How could I ever have the courage to suffer and die for love like Christ himself?

I who am so false, so unjust, so greedy, so fearful, so selfish, so proud? How idle our prattle about "believing" or "not believing" in God.

Pure speculation, and more often than not, useless.

What counts is love, and we do not know how to love, or do not wish to.

Now I understand why Paul used such forceful language when he came to the heart of the matter, and explained to the Corinthians: "If I have all the eloquence of men or of angels, but speak without love, I am simply a gong booming or a cymbal clashing. If I have the gift of prophecy, understanding all the mysteries there are, and knowing everything, and if I have faith in all its fullness, to move mountains, but without love, then I am nothing at all" (1 Cor. 13:1–2).

Here is where the real problem lies. I run the risk of being a cipher, because I do not know how to love.

So stop asking yourselves whether you believe or do not believe in God. Ask yourselves whether you do or do not love.

And if you love, forget the rest. Just love.

And love ever more and more, to the point of folly — the true folly that leads to blessedness: the folly of the cross, which is the conscious gift of self, and which possesses the most explosive force imaginable for human liberation.

That love's folly passes by way of the discovery of one's own poverty, that real poverty of not knowing how to love, is a fact. But it is also a fact that when we reach that frontier impassable to human beings, all the creative power of God steps in, and he not only says:

"Now I am making the whole of creation new" (Rev. 21:5) but adds: "I shall remove the heart of stone from your bodies and give you a heart of flesh instead" (Ezek. 36:26).

And thus, when we love, we experience God. We know God, and doubt disappears like mist in the sunshine.

— I Sought and I Found

BLESSED ARE THE MERCIFUL

Blessed are the merciful; they shall obtain mercy.

Jesus himself had difficulty in explaining what this meant, and nowhere is it said that he has been particularly successful: our poor hearts are so sick.

He said some terrible things to convince us, but his efforts were as good as wasted.

I have come across religious Sisters who would have been prepared to die as martyrs to preserve their virginity but who were not prepared to expend one ounce of goodwill to establish good working relations with a nearby convent.

I have known parents who made extreme sacrifices to provide their children with food but who could not manage to make even the smallest effort to reach agreement between themselves and stop abusing one another.

I have seen bishops spend themselves to the point of exhaustion in the service of the Church, but who could not bring themselves to go out of their "palaces" in search of the lost sheep, their primary concern being to prop up their own undisputed authority and the dignity of the Church. It might well appear from this that the gospel is no longer read, and that we have replaced it with a thousand and one other ways of interpreting our relationship with God and with our fellow men and women.

Each one of us has some object of adoration, some subject we set up on our altar; for one it will be chastity, for another the honor of the Church, and for others it will be work or economy or a good name, canon law, or a moral treatise, an old catechism or a new one, but few, all too few, are prepared to adore the loving will of Jesus, which was spelled out for us so carefully in the Father's name.

For it was Jesus himself who said to us:

> But I say this to you who are listening: love your enemies, do good to those who hate you, bless those who curse you, pray for those who treat you badly. To the man who slaps you on one cheek, present the other cheek too; to the man who takes your cloak from you, do not refuse your tunic. Give to everyone who asks you, and do not ask for your property back from the man who robs you. Treat others as you would like them to treat you. If you love those who love you, what thanks can you expect? Even sinners do that much. And if you lend to those from whom you hope to receive, what thanks can you expect? Even sinners lend to sinners to get back the same amount. Instead, love your enemies and do good, and lend without any hope of return. You will have a great reward, and you will be sons and daughters of the Most High, for he himself is kind to the ungrateful and the wicked.

Could any words express more clearly what Jesus wants of us; speak to us of the way in which God wishes us to live out our religious commitment; or explain what is God's true and innermost purpose in establishing his Church here on earth? I hardly think so...and yet?...

We are not happy because we are unforgiving, and we are unforgiving because we feel superior to others.

Mercy is the fruit of the highest degree of love, because love creates equals, and a greater love makes us inferior.

First let us establish three premises:

- Those who do not love feel superior to everyone else.

- Those who love feel equal to everyone else.

- Those who love much gladly take the lower place.

Each one of us can identify our position somewhere along this spectrum, which comprises the three degrees of the spiritual life here on earth:

- Death for those who do not love.

- Life for those who love.

- Holiness for those who love much.

The beatitude of the merciful relates, like all the beatitudes, to the realm of holiness, and we have to admit that Jesus set his sights high when he had the courage and confidence to place this lofty ideal before us. It is the beatitude that he himself lived to the full, stooping, out of love, to the lowest place, even to the extent of being rejected as a common criminal, fit only to be hung on a gibbet.

St. Paul sums it up so well in his letter to the Philippians: "His state was divine, yet he did not cling to his equality with God but emptied himself to assume the condition of a slave, and became as men are; and being as all men are, he was humbler yet, even to accepting death, death on a cross" (Phil. 2:6–7).

Rather than remaining in one or other of the three posi-
tions, which is very rare, we find ourselves straining toward
the beatitude of Jesus, moving onward toward perfection, in a
continual oscillation between death and life, between life and
holiness; experiencing the struggle between nature and grace,
the fatigue that comes from rowing with the oars of virtue, and
the unexpected joy of the wind that brings us the gifts of the
Spirit.

Anyone who is living in grace will know what I mean. . . .

Wars are fought in the name of justice and men cut each
other's throats in defense of truth, because each one has his
own truth to defend.

But Jesus' attitude is completely different, and in the end we
will simply have to come to terms with it, especially since he has
given us such an uncompromising example. Jesus went beyond
justice through love, overrode the truth by his own self-sacrifice.

He knew "what was in man." There was little to hide about
the inner reality. It was no secret that the human being is a
"scoundrel," a "cheat," a "good-for-nothing."

Jesus, in the presence of the adulteress, the prostitute, or the
thief, did not beat about the bush by saying that these men and
women were without sin.

Briefly, he did not deny the truth, but he did not stop at the
truth. He went beyond it. . . .

If God had not found the way of love when confronted with
sinful men and women, and if he had only invoked justice and
truth, how would he have overcome the great divide in order
to save us? As he died on the cross, Jesus closed the chapter of
mere justice and inaugurated on earth the authentic chapter of
"mercy."

And as the mantle of his blood falls on us, it will yield an
unparalleled fragrance, making us acceptable to the Father's
embrace. And so it is up to us now to use the same "ploy,"
the same methods, with those brothers and sisters whose gross
behavior would otherwise make it impossible for us to forgive.

From now on, whenever we encounter a thief, or a Magdalene, or a Peter, whose cowardice or deception or evil living requires our forgiveness, we will know what to do.

Instead of casting stones, and doing what his fellow Jews suggested Jesus should do with the adulteress, it will be for us to say: " 'Woman, where are they? Has no one condemned you?' 'No one, sir,' she replied. 'Neither do I condemn you,' said Jesus. 'Go away and do not sin anymore' " (John 8:11).

If we reject this way of looking at life and of interpreting the facts, we fall back on the "juridical," "inward-looking," "dead" Church, which is not in Rome, although we have become accustomed to saying so rather too glibly in order to shelve our personal responsibility, but in our own miserable hearts which, instead of listening to Jesus, go on hating, like the Pharisees of all the temples and holy places of this world.

— In Search of the Beyond

LOVE IS FOR LIVING

Having convinced myself of the primacy of charity, having become aware that in touching charity I am touching God, that in living charity I am living God in me, I must this evening, before finishing my meditation, look at tomorrow to subject it to this light and live it out under the inspiration of this synthesis of love. Basically I must do what Jesus — who brought God's love to earth and communicated it to us — would do in my position. I must remember that the opportunities I shall have to suffer, to pardon, to accept are treasures not to be lost through distraction and values that I must make my own as a worthy response to God's plan in creation.

My life is worth living if I can learn to transform everything that happens to me into love, in imitation of Jesus: because love is for living.

When I meet a brother of mine who has caused me great pain in the past by viciously calumniating me, I shall love him, and in loving him I shall transform the evil done to me into good: because love is for living.

When I have to live with people who do not see things the same way I see them, who say they are enemies of my faith, I shall love them, and in loving them I shall sow the seeds of future dialogue in my heart and theirs: because love is for living.

When I go into a shop to buy something for myself — clothes, food, or whatever it may be — I shall think of my brothers and sisters who are poorer than I am, of the hungry and the naked, and I shall use this thought to govern my purchases, trying out of love to be tight with myself and generous with them: because love is for living.

When I see time's destructive traces in my body and the approach of old age, I shall try to love even more in order to transform the coldest season of life into a total gift of myself in preparation for the imminent holocaust: because love is for living.

When I see the evening of my life, or, on the pavement in a car accident, in the agony of a fatal illness, in the ward of a geriatric hospital, feel the end coming, I shall reach out again for love, striving to accept in joy whatever fate God has had in store for me: because love is for living.

Yes, love is God in me, and if I am in love I am in God, that is, in life, in grace: a sharer in God's being. . . .

If charity is God in me, why look for God any further than myself?

And if God is in me as love, why do I change or disfigure God's face with acts or values which are not love?

— *Love Is for Living*

THE REAL SECRET

That God exists is no secret. It is clear to see!

That the human being is eternal is no secret. It is in the logic of things!

That God is good is no secret. It is the experience of every ready heart.

That God is beautiful is no secret. It is written on every flower, on the sea and on the mountains.

That God is immense is no secret. All you have to do is look at the Universe.

That God is the memory of the world is no secret. All you have to do is glance at a computer.

That God is near is no secret. You only need to look at a couple on their honeymoon, or a hen with her chicks, or two friends talking, or an expectant mother.

But then, where is the secret?

Here it is: God is a crucified God.

God is the God who allows himself to be defeated; God is the God who has revealed himself in the poor. God is the God who has washed my feet, God is Jesus of Nazareth.

We were not accustomed to a God like this.

In our childhood, the childhood of the people of God, we sought a mighty God, a God who would solve problems, a God who would eliminate the wicked, a God who would conquer enemies in a way that everyone could see.

And instead?

He appeared as a baby. He presented himself as a poor worker, not using his divinity to gain his bread.

He struck no alliances with the mighty to lord it over peoples.

He refused to leap from the pinnacle of the Temple, to work the inappropriate miracles we were expecting to make us feel more secure.

And when the ordeal came he did not run away. And he did not even get his angels to help him.

As a man, a real man, a genuine man, he accepted his sentence, shouldered his cross and trudged weeping toward the Place of the Skull to be crucified.

I have often wondered what I should have thought had I lived in Jerusalem at the time of Jesus.

Surely my mother would have sent me with him!

Off with you, follow him, go with him to chapel, go with him to the parish church.

Listen to him, stay close to him. How good he is!

And I am sure that I should have followed him gladly.

I should certainly have gathered olive branches to throw in his path that famous day of his entry into Jerusalem.

I should have clapped my hands with faith on seeing his deeds and hearing his words.

Yes, I am sure I should.

But I am just as sure that on Good Friday things would have been different.

Meanwhile my mother would be saying to me: Boy, stay at home today. Can't you see all those people in the streets? My word, what a lot of soldiers!

Don't go out. It's dangerous. Stay indoors and watch from the window.

And I should have gone to the window like any other boy, curious to know how things would turn out.

And Jesus passed right under my window. I saw him walking in chains to Calvary.

My mother would have tried to console me: Watch carefully, Carlo. Look — you'll soon see what will happen.

Jesus is the Messiah, but he is the "man of sorrows" too, as Isaiah called him (Isa. 53:3). You'll see, he'll go to his execution, but then you'll see, he won't die! You'll see, he'll come down from the cross. You'll see the angels! You'll see the miracle.

As Moses crossed the Red Sea and defeated Pharaoh, so Jesus, the new Moses, will deliver us from the executioners. He'll come down from the cross, and followed by the angels and the Zealots (they are armies — even Peter has a knife under his tunic) he'll go into the Temple and inaugurate the messianic age we've been hoping for for so long.

Watch, young sharp-eyes. Pay close attention!

What can you see, Carlo?

I can see they've nailed him to those boards! I can see him shaking his head. I can see a soldier giving him something to drink with a sponge.

Keep on looking. Don't miss anything!

Now you'll see the miracle.

And I went on looking.

What can you see?

I see that Jesus has bowed his head.

I think I heard a shout too. . . .

Mother, he's dead! Mother! He's not moving!

And my mother, like a good Jew and knowing the synagogue catechism by heart, in the face of this collapse of our messianic faith, would have said to me: "He has deceived us all. He was an impostor. Just another impostor. You see, it's impossible for the Messiah to die. Impossible!"

And what about me?

I should have said to myself: "If my mother says so. . . . But how good he was!"

Could I have kept my faith under the blow of that ordeal? I do not think so. I am no richer in faith than other people. The novelty of the Spirit was yet to come.

The new Church was yet to be born.

The secret hidden in the ages was yet to be revealed.

No one had ever imagined that life would be born from death, and that the Messiah would have reigned from the gallows. This required something more than logic, even that of all the theologians put together.

It was a revelation. And what a revelation!

Believing that henceforth we should win by losing defied all sense. Believing that God intended to inaugurate the kingdom of love freely given, the kingdom in which the poor were to be first and the rich overthrown in their uselessness and stupidity; believing in such an inversion of values would have been beyond our wildest imagination!

The Spirit had to come. And the Spirit did come. And then we believed.

Really?

Have we really believed?

Seriously believed?

Goodness! How difficult it is to believe in the sort of Messiah that Jesus of Nazareth represents!

To believe that we win by losing our very selves!

To believe that love is everything.

To believe that power is a great danger, wealth slavery, comfortable life a misfortune.

It is not easy.

This is why you hear people in the street say, "If there was a God there would not be all this suffering."

Two thousand years have gone, and there are still Christians whose doctrinal notions belong to those ancient days when the power and existence of God was revealed by displays of strength and the victory of armies. And especially by wealth and having many possessions. The real secret had not then been received.

Nor is it received very easily even today.

Hence the blasphemy in general circulation denying the kingdom's visibility, given the ordeal of suffering and death.

The old teaching that we, the Church, must be strong still feeds our determination to possess the land and dominate the world. "We must make ourselves felt. We must keep our enemies down. We must scowl. We must win, and to win we need

money, money, money. And to have money we need banks, we
need the means and we need clever bankers. How can we do
good without means, without money? Let's have a big meeting, and then any opposition will be shamed into silence. Well,
we must defend our rights, the rights of the Church. We must
defeat our enemies."

Enemies, always enemies on the Church's horizon! Yet Jesus
has told us in no uncertain terms that we no longer have any
enemies, since they are the same people we are supposed to love,
and love specially.

Can it be that we have not understood?

Don't we read the gospel in our churches?

How long shall we wait before following the teaching of
Jesus?

When shall we learn to come into a crowd dressed as Jesus
used to dress, as Francis dressed, instead of for a fashion pa-
rade, impressive and glittering like the priests in the courts of
the Temple in Jerusalem? Was nothing changed by the passage of Jesus of Nazareth? Have we made no effort to grasp
his motives for substituting humility for pride, simplicity for
complication, poverty for wealth, service for power?

Should not the holy wars, the crusades, the ranks of Christians drawn up to defend the privileges of the Church be over
and done with by now?

You see, it is hard to understand and even harder to live
the true privilege of those who follow Christ: the privilege of
the cross.

The fact of the matter is that in my old pagan heart I have
got to grasp the meaning of the Beatitudes.

They sound so unconvincing to the sort of Christians we are,
who have received baptism like the squirt of a water pistol....

And yet, in spite of us and our pagan heart, Jesus has
inaugurated the kingdom.   — *Why O Lord?*

THE WAY OF FREEDOM

The choice made by Jesus was the human being, to love humanity. It was the same as God's eternal choice: to take our part.... God is on the sinner's side, because God is on humanity's side and we are sinners.

Our sin does not nullify God's hope.

God knows that we will come back, will repent, will understand. God's faith in us is indestructible.

God is prepared to wait to the very end.

God knows that our negative element will eventually become positive, that immaturity will become maturity, sin grace, hardness gentleness, darkness light, flight return, cruelty regret, aversion embrace.

Jesus told the parable of the prodigal son with each of us in mind, knowing that each of us would live our individual version of the story. And he loves us as we are, at whatever stage of our journey.

He loves the potentiality in us.

The potentiality for conversion, return, love, light.

He loves the Magdalen when she is still a sinner, because he already sees her gradual progress toward the light as something marvelous, as something worth serious attention here on earth.

He loves Zacchaeus the sinner, robber, exploiter, and finds it good that such a man can be capable of reversing his conduct and becoming a friend to the poor.

Yes, God loves what in us is not yet.

What has still to come to birth.

What we love in a person is what already is: virtue, beauty, courage, and hence our love is self-interested and fragile.

God, loving what is not yet and putting faith in us, continually begets us, since love is what begets.

By giving us confidence, God helps us to be born, since love is what helps us to emerge from our darkness and draws us to the light.

And this is such a fine thing to do that God invites us to do the same.

The charity that God transmits to us is this very ability to love things in a person that do not as yet exist.

For me to love my neighbor's negative element is disinterested love.

To love him in his poverty, in his lies, in his impurity, in his duplicity, in his darkness.

And love, swooping down on him, has the power to regenerate him.

Love creates the divine environment for us, making transformation possible.

By feeling ourselves loved, we are prompted to set out on the way of salvation.

Our poverty shrivels up, our lies become odious to us, our impurity becomes a yearning for purity, our darkness is invaded by light.

When Jesus tells me, "Love your enemy," he indicates the maximum possibility and capacity for loving; and at the same time he offers me the maximum hope of having peace on earth. By besieging my enemy with love and not with weapons, I facilitate in him and in myself the possibility of seeing that day dawn when "calf and lion-cub will feed together and a child will put his hand into the viper's lair, and none will harm the other" (see Isa. 11:6–9).

By my exertions, I expand the kingdom promised us and enter my heritage of peace.

Yes, loving the negative in humanity.

Loving it in the certainty that tomorrow the positive will prevail. Seen like this, the world no longer frightens me.

Seeing the city like this, I feel a hearty desire to act and to hope. Before I understood these things, sin filled me with repulsion; I thought of it as an enemy.

By the same token, I felt friendly toward the police who arrested prostitutes and willingly preached on the perils of hell-fire to frighten the lads — to put the fear of God in them.

But now the sinner fills me with compassion; if I run into a prostitute I offer her a coffee; I have more hope in salvation, and the compassion that I feel for the sufferings of humankind is so intense that I utter the word "hell" far less often.

You might say — and this gives me intense and heart-felt joy — that I feel myself a friend to all, I am no longer upset when I meet someone who doesn't believe in God, I am more surprised when the opposite occurs; I cannot not belong to a sinful church. When I run into some "right-minded" person of the old moralizing type, I realize how the Church's slow progress is due to lack of confidence in the coming generations and to the assumption that the old days exemplified the only way in which things should be done.

Yes, loving the negative in human beings, loving what is not yet in them.

Those who have "given up all hope" for Christianity are precisely those who only want to see the positive in human beings and set no value on the negative.

This is why they suffer.

How could they not suffer at the sight of such disorder.

I admit it: the world is a terrible sight today if only seen in the light of what goes on: if not seen in the light of our hope that God overcomes evil.

The city seen from its positive side represents God's defeat.

The Church seen from the same point of view looks as though she's done for.

But seeing things like this and talking of them like this, I basically deny God's mysterious activity: God acts, transforms, gives life, brings to the light.

If the world is, as St. Paul says, in the pangs of childbirth, how can I not regard the negative aspect that I now see as a hope of what will be?

Yes, we should affirm this clearly.

He has no faith in God who only believes in his own actions, who only believes in what can be seen; he does not believe in the mystery, in God's potentiality, in God's invincible presence in history, in evolution.

In his heart, he does not believe in the parable of the prodigal son, for this is the parable of all humankind collectively, and hence of the victory of good over evil (see Luke 15).

— Summoned by Love

PRAY, LOVE, WAIT

I should like to teach you a little trick: just the thing for someone afraid of suffering — or better still for someone trying to suffer less.

The trick is this: LOVE MORE TO SUFFER LESS.

I have tried this many a time! And although I am still taking my first steps, I can see that it works.

And I intend to get it perfect, this trick of mine, because suffering always takes us by surprise, and we feel a great need of a little respite when the ordeal overtakes us! Now that I am old I have plenty of opportunity for doing this. Listen.

The Germans, and even more the Austrians, have a great love of candles — beautiful brightly colored candles with different kinds of symbols and lettering on them. They make absolute masterpieces for putting on the table on a holiday, or on the altar as a sign of joy and communion.

You know the meaning of candles in church — what they symbolize.

They originate from the Passover night, the Pasch of the Lord. The first Christians used the candle to symbolize Christ's presence in the darkness of the world.

As Christ is the light of the world and was consumed by love, so also this candle gives light by burning itself away.

It is a sign, and like all signs it has a message for us.

It has said much to me. I have watched it gleaming afar on Holy Saturday night. I have made it mine when celebrating Easter Sunday Mass in community, beginning with the short ceremony of the light.

But I have gone a little further in understanding about the light that consumes the wax.

And when a dear friend of mine in Vienna presented me with one of these colored candles I took it home to my cell and put it on my chest of drawers next to a little icon.

And now I have something like a little altar.

And now I should like to explain the trick I use.

When sorrows come upon me, as happens fairly often, and I feel as though I am down a dark hole, I light the candle. Gazing at it I try to repeat the words I find so easy to say during our public ceremony of the light of Christ.

"Do you see this candle? It is the symbol of Jesus who gives light to the world by being consumed, as this candle is consumed."

Now let me say right from the start that to say this to others is easier than saying it to yourself.

But I say it and try to take courage.

And then what do I do?

Continuing my little personal liturgy, I do three things.

Little things that have occurred to me, leading in the right direction.

I pray.

I love.

I wait.

As for praying, this is not the moment to come out with some magnificent speech to God.

I just say a prayer appropriate to a poor man like myself, and every time I say it I like it better because it is simple and says it all in a few words.

When I feel like that I love this prayer. I say it once for every bead of the rosary I am holding. Here it is! "Help comes to me from Yahweh, who made heaven and earth" (Ps. 121:2).

Then I remind myself: calling for help is not enough, praying is not enough. As Jesus has told us, it is not those who keep saying, "Lord, Lord," who will enter the kingdom of heaven (Matt. 7:21; see also Luke 6:46).

That is too easy. One must do more.

And doing more brings us back to the same theme I have been repeating over and over throughout this book, at the risk of boring you:

Love, Carlo.

Make an effort in the right direction: in the direction of Christ the lover.

I rarely feel that I have no reason to love.

I have long known that if I want to be happy on earth I must fall madly in love with God and the things of God.

Then, all things being equal, in time of suffering the easiest way to allay the suffering, especially if it is really sharp, is to get out of myself yes, get out of myself, visit someone who is suffering worse than I am, do something to remind me of the sufferings of the world, set my heart in order if I feel a residual dislike of someone, write a check for the world's poorest mission, answer a tiresome letter from someone who wants me to tell him whether hell exists, or what he should not do to leave his nasty, possessive wife.

In other words, perform an act of love that requires patience and honesty.

If I were younger I should willingly go out and spend an hour playing cards with an old-age pensioner living alone and dying of loneliness. I should take the opportunity of emptying his chamber pot and dabbing a drop of scent on his sheets.

That done, what else is to be done as the candle goes on burning itself away?

One very simple thing. But something very real and very necessary.

Wait.

And while I am waiting that passage from Scripture always comes to mind: "It is good to wait in silence for Yahweh to save" (Lam. 3:26).

Then I usually fall asleep, so I don't know what happens next. But at last I feel better.   — *Why O Lord?*

4

The Church of Sinners

A ROBBERS' DEN...

How much I must criticize you, my Church, and yet how much I love you!

How you have made me suffer and yet how much I owe you.

I should like to see you destroyed and yet I need your presence. You have given me so much scandal and yet you have made me understand holiness.

Never in the world have I seen anything more obscurantist, more compromised, more false, yet never have I touched anything more pure, more generous, or more beautiful.

How often I have felt like slamming the door of my soul in your face — and how often I have prayed that I might die in your sure arms!

No, I cannot be free of you, for I am one with you, even though not completely you.

Then, too — where should I go? To build another?

But I cannot build another without the same defects, for they are my own defects I bear within me. And again, if I build one, it will be my Church, and no longer Christ's.

I am old enough to know that I am no better than others.

The other day a friend of mine wrote a letter to a newspaper. "I am leaving the Church," he said. "It is so involved with the rich that it has lost its credibility."

That hurts me. Either this person is a sentimentalist, without experience of life, and then I can excuse him — or he is proud, someone who thinks himself better than others, thinks himself more credible than others.

None of us is credible while we are on this earth.

"You think me a saint!" St. Francis shouted. "And do you know, I can still beget children on a prostitute if Christ support me not!" Credibility is not a human attribute. It is God's alone, and Christ's. The human attribute is weakness and, every once in a while, the good will to do something good with the help of the grace that spurts from the invisible veins of the visible Church.

Was yesterday's Church any better than today's? Was the Church of Jerusalem any more "credible" than the Roman?

When Paul arrived in Jerusalem, bearing in his heart his thirst for universality, on the mighty wind of charismatic inspiration, might not the discourses of James on foreskins to be amputated, or the weakness of Peter who was dallying with the rich of those days (the sons and daughters of Abraham) and who gave scandal by dining only with the pure — might not these have given him doubts about the truth of the Church, which Christ had founded fresh as the morning, and made him feel like going off to found another one at Antioch or Tarsus?

Might not St. Catherine of Siena, seeing the pope intriguing against her city (and a dirty intrigue it was), the city of her heart, have suddenly decided to take to the Sienese hills, those hills crystalline as the skies, and fashion another Church more crystalline than the Roman, so opaque and obtuse, so sinful, so political?

No, I think not. Both Paul and Catherine knew how to distinguish between the people who composed the Church, the Church's "personnel," as Maritain called them — and that human society called "Church," which, unlike all other human societies, "has received from God a personality that is supernatural, holy, immaculate, pure, indefectible, infallible, beloved of Christ as his spouse, and worthy to be loved by myself as my most sweet mother."

Here is the mystery of the Church of Christ, the true, impenetrable mystery.

The Church has the power to give me holiness, and it is composed entirely of sinners, each and every member of it. Some sinners!

It has the all-powerful, invincible faith to celebrate the eucharistic mystery ever and again, and it is composed of weak men and women groping in the dark and daily grappling with the temptation to lose faith.

It bears a message of purest ray serene and is incarnate in a dough as dirty as the world is dirty.

It speaks of the Master's sweetness and nonviolence, yet has sent armies to disembowel infidels and torture heretics.

It transmits a message of evangelical poverty, and does nothing but collect money and strike alliances with the mighty.

One has only to read the proceedings in the trial of St. Joan of Arc at the hands of the Inquisition to be assured that Stalin was not the first to falsify documents and to prostitute judges.

One has only to think of what was done to innocent Galileo to make him sign under duress, to be assured that, however much they may be Church, the people of the Church, the Church's personnel, are evil people, the cheapest personnel that can be had, capable of committing errors as vast as the earth's orbit round the sun.

In vain do we look for anything else from the Church, other than this mystery of infallibility and fallibility, of sanctity and sin, of weakness and courage, of credibility and non-credibility.

Those who dream of anything else but this are only wasting their time and always having to start again. Furthermore, they demonstrate their failure to understand human beings.

For this is the way human beings are — just as the Church shows them to be — in their wickedness, yet in that invincible courage which faith in Christ has bestowed on them and with which the charity of Christ fortifies their lives.

When I was young, I did not understand why, in spite of Peter's denial, Jesus still wanted him to be the head of the Church, his successor, the first pope. Now I am no longer surprised. I have gradually come to understand that the founding of the Church on the tomb of a traitor, a person terrified by a servant-girl's chatter, is a permanent warning for each of us to stay humble and aware of our own frailty.

No, I shall not leave this Church, founded on so frail a rock, because I should be founding another one on an even frailer rock: myself.

And then, what do rocks matter? What matters is Christ's promise, what matters is the cement that binds the rocks into one: the Holy Spirit. The Holy Spirit alone can build the Church with stones as ill-hewn as we!

The Holy Spirit alone can hold us together, keep us one in spite of ourselves, in spite of the centrifugal force with which our boundless pride endows us.

For myself, when I hear the Church being criticized, I am pleased. I listen as I would to a serious, reflective sermon inspired by a thirst for the good, and a clear, untrammeled vision of things.

"We ought to be poor ... evangelical ... we ought not to rely on alliances with the powerful," and so forth and so on. But in the end, I feel this criticism, leveled against the person of my parish priest, my bishop, or my pope, is actually addressed to me. I feel that I am in the same boat, in the same barque of Peter — blood relative that I am to certified sinners and a sinner myself.

And then I try to criticize myself, and perceive how difficult conversion is. . . .

No, it is not wicked to criticize the Church when you love it. It is wicked to criticize it from outside, as though you yourself were pure. It is not wicked to criticize the sin and the ugly things we see. It is wicked to saddle others with them, while believing ourselves to be innocent, poor, and meek.

This is wicked. . . .

But what have all these considerations to do with the Church? Friends, there is a connection. I mention all these things because they have a close connection with our considerations on the Church. A very close connection!

This is one of the discoveries I have made in my long experience of life, something important I have found.

I have found, I have discovered, that the Church is not divided from the world. The Church is the world's soul, the world's conscience, the world's heaven. Precisely because Christ became incarnate, I no longer have the right to divide the good from the bad, the innocent from the wicked, Zacchaeus from Peter, the adulteress from the apostles.

All are a single whole called the Church. And Jesus died for the Church, and Jesus and the Church are functions of each other.

The people of God are a people of saints, prophets and priests, and at the same time a people of sinners, adulterers, and tax-gatherers.

When I was a boy, I looked on the Church as separate from the world.

Now I see the Church quite differently.

And on careful thought, I have to admit that the reason I see it differently is that I have learned to see myself differently.

This is where the mystery lies.

This hodge-podge of good and bad, greatness and wretchedness, sanctity and sin, this Church-World, is, at bottom: me.

In me, there is everything. In me lives the world, and the Church.

In me, there is capacity for evil and the yearning for holiness; corrupt nature and sanctifying grace.

In me, there is Adam and there is Christ.

And as all these are in me, so all these things are in others. It is the mystery of Church-World.

The deed of the Father has made me a "house of prayer"; my own devilish deeds have succeeded in turning it into a "den of thieves."

Which being the case . . . many things will have to be changed. Which being the case, I, the Church in my visible form, must present a different face to the world.

· I must not present myself to sinners as holy, to the unjust as just, to the impure as pure.

I must be careful not to be too hasty in climbing onto my soap box and preaching to others, or so confidently giving them my brilliant instructions.

It is hard to separate Adam's sin within me from the transparency of Jesus' prophecy there.

It is pride to feel safe and secure in this "house of prayer" and take no account of Christ's reproach, " . . . you have turned it into a robbers' den" (Mark 11:17).

Do not let us hesitate to say this — Christ's fearsome words against the Temple in Jerusalem applied not only to the Temple, then intent on putting him to death, but to every one of us and every one of our parish churches. Every one of us can become a den of thieves, and so can every one of our churches.

By what authority do we think that, because Jesus has come, we are simply no longer capable of sin, or that the Church no longer runs the risk of putting revenue before prayer?

Well, then?

What am I to do?

My feeling is, the first thing I must do is change my attitude.

If it is true that sin and holiness cohabit in me and I cannot separate what the Church is from what the world is, I ought to be more humble in my attitude toward things going on around me. In future, I must not be so ready to judge others as vessels of the world's sin and feel myself to be ever-innocent because I belong to the Church. . . .   — I Sought and I Found

•

I would like to be pope for just one day! I may be mistaken, but what joy I would feel if I sold the whole Vatican to the highest bidder and went to live in a little apartment on the outskirts of the city, or better still, in a tent between the desert and the steppe.

Utopia?

Of course, but a utopia that does good like all the utopias of the gospel.

And the young would be so ready for utopia!

Especially today.

It may be that the idea of selling the Vatican and its museums so as to transform the resulting space into leper villages has filled you with enthusiasm, as it has me.

But do you want to understand the illogicality of our enthusiasm, or rather the injustice of it?

This evening, when I was thinking not about other people's things but my own, I noticed that my little room was warmer than the room of the brothers with whom I live, the bed softer, my life in general more comfortable.

For one reason or another I am always at the head of the line, and I always leave the last place to the weakest and most silent.

This means that if I were pope, even for just one day, I wouldn't do a single thing to implement my ideas.

In the Church it is all too easy to ask others to make great prophetic gestures, to embrace poverty, to share possessions.

The difficult thing is to ask it of ourselves, to live it ourselves.

I recall a Latin American writer, one famous for his fine writing and protests about torture and social injustice and the necessity of revolution.

He himself told me that when it came to the crunch, when he was in danger of being arrested after a military coup, he fled from his country on the first airplane, carrying with him the shame of his cowardice, because he knew full well that he had left behind him the poorest and least protected.

Brothers, it is difficult to bear witness.

And it is precisely when we feel incapable of doing this that we risk hiding ourselves behind fine words!

Listen to the intentions formulated during the prayer of the faithful in the various church groups we belong to. You would think we were all heroes, all determined to divest the Church of her riches.

Then let us look at ourselves to see whether our actions correspond to our words.

Where have we got to in the matter of sharing our possessions?

And is it for this reason that, not wanting to be rhetorical, I ought to say this evening, not "If I were pope," but "If I were Brother Carlo, what would I now do to make the gospel actual in my life?"

What ought I to do in practical terms if I want to respond to Jesus when he says to me, as he said to Zacchaeus, "Make haste and come down, for I must stay at your house today?" (Luke 19:5).   *— The Desert in the City*

PEOPLE OF GOD

St. Laurent, November 25, 1962

My dearest sister,

...In one of your last letters you said you were worried about me, that you had noticed something new in me. It may be, my dear, that the Lord is preparing something new for me. It is certain that I have felt as never before that earthly life no longer matters to me. These are difficult things to talk about. It's not that I don't value God's gift contained in every twenty-four hours of life down here, but...it seems I have grasped something else and the horizon down here no longer attracts me the way it used to do. I seem to have run my course.

But we shall see.

I've also got another reason for feeling "Nunc dimittis": the historic importance of the Council. I have longed so much for twenty years that something should come about in the Church to change things! I have really suffered. And now I think that it has happened, that spring is knocking at the door, that the polemic between the Church and the world is silent for a moment, that the oldest and most reactionary situations are opening up and . . . so many other things are happening!

What happiness, my sister!

And how true it is that it is God who acts, not us.

Who would have thought of such a thing at the close of Pius XII's pontificate? It was the Almighty preparing the ground for future sowing.

So . . . don't worry! I'm not depressed. Instead I'm more aware than I used to be, more at peace, but as though on the eve of something, and you know that vigil vestments are not white or red, but *purple*. . . .   — *Letters to Dolcidia*

•

On the subject of the Church as community: . . .

It's no good sheltering in the old refrain: "It's not my concern. . . . I can't do anything about it . . . it's the priest's concern, the bishop's concern, my mother's concern."

I think it's everybody's concern.

The first symptom of conversion by which we prove that we have grasped what the Church actually is, is when we stop thinking about the Church as being only the Vatican or the diocese and think of it as being each one of us.

We are the Church!

Each of us is the Church!

What power would be generated were all Christians to keep saying, and each to contribute something to the activities of the bishop by saying, "It concerns me."

Now I am making a start.

Now I am trying to make a community.

I don't want to be on my own any more.

I want to have companions on my journey.

To live my life with them.

Even if there are only a few of us,
I want to make a start.
We shall pray at home.
We shall read the Bible together.
We shall make the Eucharist what the first Christians made it.
We shall hale each other.
We shall pool as much of our property as we can.
We shall live by the gospel.

And I think that the acutely worrying problem of priestly vocations would soon be solved in a community of this sort.

A community of prayer.

A community-Church in which the faith is sincerely lived automatically becomes a seminary. Where the Word is proclaimed, the Spirit comes, and the task of the Spirit is to make a Church and distribute its graces within it.

I am absolutely convinced that the grace of the priesthood will manifest itself forthwith in any such community of mature faith and prayer — far sooner indeed than in those wan and anemic colleges kept open merely for fear that vocations may dry up. Communities born alive and fecund in our own day...have no problems as regards vocations. They have as many priests as they want and doubtless some to spare. So why be afraid?

God is God and will not let his Church want for the necessary shepherds.   — *Summoned by Love*

CALLED TO SERVE

When I was in the desert I earned my daily bread as a meteorologist. My work consisted in visiting five stations I had set up, which recorded data on temperature, humidity, wind direction and velocity, rainfall — things like that.

It was interesting work, and it earned me the wherewithal to travel the desert trails, where I found Tuareg encampments, work camps, uranium and diamond prospectors, and, most valued of all, wells of sweet water.

For some time I had been in contact with a Swedish engineer, who had been converted to Catholicism and whom I had been meeting and instructing for about two years. Now he wanted me to baptize him, on his work site, among his colleagues, in a work camp of prospectors for precious minerals, between Ideles and Djanet.

On my way through Laghouat, the center of the diocese, I asked and received the bishop's permission to do this, and, in high heart, fixed the date for the ceremony that Alex, the neophyte, wanted.

The stage seemed set for a magnificent demonstration of faith in that lost region of the Sahara.

On the date agreed, as though drawn there by grace and friendship, geographers, prospectors, doctors, from camps hundreds of miles away all round, agreed to meet in this wild, lonely place in the desert called Tabelbella....

Inside the tent where we gathered next evening for Alex's baptism, there was as interesting a congregation as ever I could wish to see.

What surprised me was that we were all practicing Christians, and that nearly all had been members of militant movements such as the Young Christian Workers, the Belgian Student Youth, the Focolare, the Neo-Catechumenal Way communities, and family spirituality movements.

The Holy Spirit descended on us, gathered there as the Church, and when I poured the water over Alex's head there was general emotion, and the joy of all was plain to see.

Then we sat down and each in turn spoke of his or her pilgrimage in the faith.

I was impressed by the maturity of these people, who had gone out there to work, certainly, but most of all for an ideal they had acquired.... When everyone had finished telling the story of their lives, there was a moment of silence in the tent.

The Spirit's fire had welded us into a unity. Emotion was strong and visible. Now it was my turn to say something.

I felt small and unworthy among these mature people, experts at their work, educated people who had traveled a long, hard road.

I extricated myself by asking a question, which seemed to me both mature and valid.

"What is missing in this tent? We are gathered here as a community of faith. We have prayed together. As though we were early Christians, we have received one of our number into the Church, who from now on will walk in faith, trying to live in imitation of Jesus, our Lord and Teacher.

"But what is missing in this tent? Tell me!"

A voice, Francesco's, broke the silence: "The Eucharist. The presence of Jesus under the sign he left us at the Last Supper."

I said nothing.

Never had I felt as at that moment the historical absurdity of a community of Christians deprived of the Eucharist for the sole reason that no priest was present.

But the priest was far away. It had been many months since these prospectors had received Communion, for lack of priests. All were militant Christians, conscientious about their faith, and it was only because their work and their duties had taken them so far away that they were forced to live without the Eucharist for months on end.

In that tent, and seeing that community gathered there, hundreds of miles from the nearest mission — I realized that the situation was really unjustifiable. Why? Why did communities in Zaire or Equatorial Guinea, made up of excellent Christians instructed by their African catechists, have to go without the Eucharist simply because they had no priest?

Why did they have no priest? Because those people were all married, and the Church only ordained celibates.

Could it really be that celibacy should constitute the absolute sine qua non?

Could it really be that merely being married debarred one from consecrating the Body of the Lord in the assembly of the faithful?

Was this what Jesus commanded?

Was being married so great a defect as to rule out the possibility of becoming a priest in Christ's Church?

No, no, there was something wrong here! Something amiss in the Church's attitude today.

Clearly, it was the weight of a past already over and done, and it would have to be faced up to. It was obedience to an outmoded historical situation, which continued to operate by exploiting either the indolence of the faithful, which is great, or the mysterious power that taboos have in age-old traditions and myth-based cultures.

What had Jesus' will been in instituting the Eucharist?

Had he commanded celibacy, or had he commanded, "Do this in memory of me?"

Had not the will to celibacy, driven to the most improbable extremes in recent centuries, especially by religious, ended by distorting the very will of Christ?

Between an obligatory celibacy reducing the number of priests and the need not to have the community without the Eucharist, which is the right choice to make?

Hasn't the community a right to the Eucharist?

Why deny it to them merely because they have no celibate willing to be a priest?

Once I saw a letter, written by an African, an exemplary Christian and father, to his bishop, which read more or less as follows:

Father Bishop:

I should like to ask you a favor. Our village is entirely Christian, but it is very, very small. And it will never be able to have a permanent priest to celebrate daily Mass, as we should like.

Sometimes we have to wait for months before having the joy of Mass.

Father Bishop, we have our catechist among us. He is married, he is good, he is rich in faith and charity. Why not ask the pope to give you the power to ordain him a priest.

This way we shall always have the Eucharist.

What answer can be given to this poor Christian?

What logical reasons are there for refusing his request?

Is it enough, everlastingly, to repeat that the priesthood can be conferred only on celibates?

Why not on married people as well?

Is there any prohibition in Scripture?

What was done in the primitive Church?

How were things managed in the early centuries?

Or perhaps haven't we, whether by historical necessity or because of our celibate tastes, changed the order of things? I think so.

I speak as a celibate, from a celibacy given me by God himself as an irreversible charism.

I discern in myself no other alternative in life and have such joy in my body by reason of this gift entrusted to me by the Lord that I venture to say, with Paul, "Brothers and sisters, I wish you were all like me."

But with just as much force and awareness, I tell you that I could wish to have received the Eucharist from my father, who was well worthy of being a priest even though he was married.

With just as much hope, I assure you that we are on the eve of a time when the Church will stop making the customary speeches about the shortage of priests today, because these speeches are not true. There is no shortage of priests today.

We have all we need, and more than we need — as always, thanks to God's generous provision for us.

But they are to be found among married people, and that is where the Church should look for them.

What a change it will be to stop feeling worried about the shortage of priests in the Church!

What a joy it will be when the Church at large realizes that things have changed, and that the closing of the seminaries for celibates only, which God himself has emptied, has been a grace, one of the greatest graces of post-Conciliar times.

If I may be allowed to say so!...When I saw the seminaries and novitiates emptying after the pontificate of Pius XII, I was literally terrified. Then, as Jesus invites us to do in such cases, I prayed.

And that was when I seemed to understand, confusedly at first, but then more and more clearly, that with a phenomenon so vast we ought to look more closely, and see whether, down deep, there isn't something that God is trying to tell his Church.

It was not a question of this or that seminary, of this or that region, but of all the seminaries. The whole Church was afflicted with the same problem.

When I think how my cardinal spent ten years of work — and what work! — bleeding the diocese to build a seminary which looked like a tourist village and then found it empty almost as soon as it was finished, I said to myself, in my incurable simplicity: "Either God is playing a joke on us, or he means to teach us a lesson we won't forget!"

And when I saw new, empty seminaries in Rovigo, Bologna, Santo Lussurgiu, Assisi, Fermo, Brescia, Turin, Verona, Vicenza, and so on...!

I do not believe the Lord would wish to play jokes on his Church. No, he must have wished to say, in a somewhat blunt way, that it ought to change vocation strategy.

For it is unthinkable that God would want to leave the Church without priests.

It would be a serious lack of faith to think that.

Let us not forget: the priest is bound to the eucharistic mystery, and I cannot do without the Eucharist.

Well, then?

Well, then I became convinced that the simultaneous closing of all the seminaries was only an "organizational problem," due to the unforeseeable strategy of the Spirit.

Yes, I am convinced: God has personally emptied the seminaries because he wants something else. And we must look for this something else in simplicity of heart and freedom of spirit.

Above all, I think God no longer wants obligatory celibacy.

I believe in celibacy too much to see it reduced to such a sorry state. And there is only one way to save it: leave it to free choice, humbly begging it as a gift from above, as a charism that only the God of the impossible can give.

The day the choice is free, and the priesthood is possible in either state, the number of celibates will increase, since the Church will have proved that it does not place its trust in itself and attribute to itself, as heretofore, the power to create celibates, but looks for them to God alone.

And if grace so abounds as to produce in the Church the miracle of enough celibates to assure the priestly ministry, we shall certainly sing the Magnificat. But we shall never return — and this is basic to the spirituality of marriage — we shall never return to the notion that when one gets married one becomes a mediocre Christian....

Thank you, Francis, who by not being a ministerial priest yourself helped me to understand that I too could be a priest in a genuine, theological sense, without being one in the ministerial sense.

Because I too went through this crisis and did not want to be ordained a priest.

For different reasons, I admit. Reasons that were authentic signs of my own times.

Not, certainly, out of humility. I did not want to be a priest for reasons to do with the apostolate. I got my training during the pontificate of Pius XII, when, under the impulse of Catholic

Action, the laity began to be aware of their dignity in the service of the Church.

This was the great inspiration of Pope Pacelli [John XXIII], a pope particularly sensitive to the dignity of the laity and to their involvement in the field of the apostolate.

It was an epic breakthrough for us, and each of us felt understood and helped.

It was then, right then, during my time in Catholic Action, that I decided not to be ordained a priest, thus leaving me free to proclaim, in lay clothes, to the laity as yet ignorant and unaware, that the Church was the Church of all, and not only of the priests — as the parishes of that time largely gave the impression.

We were all part of the Church, and all had to feel that the Church belonged to us, and work at spreading the kingdom by our own activity, which was beginning to take on the face of an authentic personal vocation.

These were marvelous times, and I thank God for letting me live in them.

I must, however, say that we had not yet fulfilled our aim. We were still on the way.

Fulfillment was to come with the Council.

What an illumination for all of us it was, when the Council stood the theology of the Church on its head in its efforts to "rethink itself as Church," as Pope John liked to put it, and later defined itself so clearly with Pope Paul.

The Church was a clerical pyramid no more. It was the people of God, marching through the desert; a society of faith and prayer, in which each one had his place; the mystery of Christ alive in history, the people whom Christ had won by his blood and to whom he had transmitted, by his Spirit on Calvary, holiness, prophecy and priesthood.

It was the Church of the new age.

The new age has arrived, and it is ours....

— I Sought and I Found

TOLERANCE

Spello, June 1974

Dearest Sisters and dear Piero,*

If there is one thing for which we ought to thank the Lord, it is that of being born into a genuine Christian community. When I think of Papa and Mamma and what they did to bring us up in the faith, I end up lost for words with which to say thank you to the Lord for the gifts showered upon us.

And I found myself in the desert as though it were a second period of my life, to empty myself of my securities and free myself from idols. It has been the most splendid adventure of my life, even if it has been the roughest and most painful.

Things can be seen more clearly from the desert and in a more eternal perspective. The cosmos takes the place of your country of birth and God becomes a real absolute. Even the Church takes on the wider dimensions of the universe and "those far away," that is, those who are not yet visibly Christians become neighbors.

I ended up on Islamic soil just as you, Piero, had meanwhile become bishop in a Buddhist country.

The first lesson you learn when you love non-Christians is tolerance. Little by little your arrogant wish to lay down the law to others fades away and you end up feeling yourself a poor exile in a foreign land. There's another thing you learn from those who don't share your faith: that God is their God and isn't waiting for you in order to reach them with his spirit which is love.

In this way the boundaries of the Church are infinitely extended and you live in the comfort of thinking how Jesus died for all and has already touched all with his supreme sacrifice.

---

*In a referendum in Italy, Carretto publicly aligned himself with those seeking to overturn the ban on civil divorce. Thousands of indignant protests followed. Here he tried to explain his position to his family. Piero was Carlo's brother, a Salesian priest who served as a missionary — and eventually bishop — in Thailand.

The time will come when they too will join the visible Church, but potentially they are already there, and you ought to adopt an attitude of great respect and love toward them.

And above all you must not judge them, as Jesus taught us. These things came back into my thoughts just recently when, without wanting to, I found myself in the whirlwind of the referendum.

I know that I have scandalized you and this is why it was right that I should write to explain myself to you whom I love.

My God! How awful is the thought of causing suffering to those you love! What agony I had at the time! Thinking that I was a cause of division for thousands of my brothers and sisters with whom I had prayed in liturgical assemblies and with whom I had broken the Bread of life has been an intolerable hurt.

But it was the truth that upheld me and "set me free" even in the jaws of death and frightful contradictions.

And what is this truth?

It is the truth that blossomed and flowered from the root of my vocation as a Little Brother and yours, dear Piero, as a bishop among the Buddhists of Thailand. It is the truth of tolerance.

It is the truth that in the post-Conciliar Church something radically different has been introduced into our history.

Buddhism for you, and Islam for me, have taught us to live in a foreign country no longer as masters but as exiles, and to understand in depth those who do not yet share our own faith.

But you will tell me: here we're in Italy. Yes, we're in Italy, but is Italy still Christendom? No. This is one of the most obvious signs of the times which we ought to grasp: Italy is a jumble of ideologies, a mission country, a land where Christians (not by baptism, but by faith) are becoming a minority.

So this is the real problem posed by the divorce referendum: is it the indissolubility of marriage that is in question, or respect for those who do not share the faith?

In conscience I have no doubts in this regard.

None of us Christians can cast doubt on Jesus' own words: "What God has joined together let no one put asunder," but these words cannot be used as a civil law for those who do not believe in Christ's resurrection and belong to a secular society.

I am well aware that indissolubility is the perfection of marriage and the truest proposal that Christians can put before non-Christians, but can I impose it with a law on those who — much more so than our fathers — have a "stiff neck"? *Conscience had to answer this question; some answered yes, others answered no. I think that both are in the Church and had the right to express themselves.*

Our pastors' directives were a guide but were not binding in conscience.

It's useless for us who know each other to affirm our love for the Church: I think that all five of us are willing to die for it, and we have given witness to that.

I'd like to end this letter of mine by supporting my case with an example which touches us close to home, even though the example only concerns the merciful manner in which the Church deals with those who have fallen short, while the indissolubility of marriage is something else.

You know how the Church is suffering at this time because of those who are leaving the priesthood or the religious life. It's a phenomenon on an awful scale which involves tens of thousands of priests and Sisters.

Well then, what is the post-Conciliar Church doing? Whereas at one time it left defrocked priests excommunicated in a corner without the comfort of the sacraments until on the point of death, it has now as it were understood the gospel more profoundly, even realizing that it was mistaken, and it opens its arms to them, readmits them to communion, and gives them hope. And the same thing happens to the thousands of Sisters who have abandoned their vows. Mercy takes the place of justice and the Church shows itself to be a force for freedom to those who have fallen outside the law.

Can you feel that there's something new in the air? The gospel is knocking as never before at the doors of a world racked by violence, disorder, and sin. As Christians we have to present ourselves as the bearers, not of a religion crippled by time and our sins, but of the breath of a gospel which is love, mercy, and newness. Listen to the words of Pope John on his deathbed: "Now more than ever, and certainly more than in centuries gone by, we are committed to serving humanity as such and not just Catholics; to defending first of all and everywhere the rights of the human person and not just those of the Catholic Church. It's not that the gospel is changing, but we are beginning to understand it better."

I'd like to leave you with these words and tell you of all the love which binds me to you.

Love,

Carlo

•

Spello, December 2, 1974

Dear Dolce,

But is it possible that I never get anything right with you anymore!!! I'm sorry to have made you suffer again over the affair of the married clergy. I only said what some of the African bishops said at the October Synod. *Where there are no more priests do you prefer no longer to receive the Eucharist* or to accept that the Church should ordain married men? I would willingly have received Communion from Papa. But aren't you aware that you are a slave to fantasies!!! Wasn't St. Peter married? I can understand that a celibate priest is better, and *in fact I have chosen celibacy,* but I would not be scandalized to see the father of a family celebrating the Eucharist.

Besides, if you live a few years longer — less than five — you'll see it in practice in the Church.

But why should we get angry about things which don't matter? Poor Dolce! I'm sorry to see you like this. I wish that when you considered the faith you referred more to apostolic times than to the pontificate of Pius XII.

I love you.

Now I'm in silence here in the hermitage. I'm working on my new book, *Summoned by Love.*

I know you don't trust me anymore, but I'm telling you all the same: pray for this new book of mine.

It's all about confidence in God. I hope you'll like it.

Love,

Carlo

•

Spello, January 22, 1975

Dear Dolce,

You are indeed on the pope's side, and you do right to say so. *But what makes you think that I'm not?*

The problem is this. I can be on the pope's side even if I disagree with him about things not concerning the faith. *I was on Pope Pius XII's side, but I had the courage to tell him that the Latin Mass had to be changed; that Franco was not treating the workers well in Spain; that the seminaries needed changing, etc., etc.* This is what I mean when I talk about fanaticism.

I can have different ideas from my bishop about things which concern the civil law and the *Referendum law was a civil, not a religious law.*

Nobody can convince me that to be tolerant of an atheist is to be against the gospel. *I tolerate the divorce* of a nonbeliever, I do not desire it.

Fanatic means being unwilling to seek out the truth but considering yourself already the possessor of truth without thinking it through.

Everybody can say silly things, even the bishops, and we should make sure that our obedience is an informed obedience.

Do you know what Cardinal Newman said? "I will never obey an order which is against my conscience." Read the gospel. How many times does Jesus disobey the Temple? Was he disobedient or was it the Temple that was no longer in the right?

It's all a mess, you see, and it was brought about by one single mistake: *The bishops couldn't order what they ordered; they could only advise.* Can you understand it? I love you and don't worry.

Carlo

— *Letters to Dolcidia*

WOMEN'S GIFTS

Strange. I have asked myself many times how it is possible that, in spite of personages as remarkable as Clare, as Catherine, as Teresa, you in the Church are still so antifeminist?

Yes, I have to say it, I, Francis.* You are still antifeminist.

I cannot understand!

Have you fear of a woman because a woman endangers your virtue? Or do you consider her, without openly saying so, as belonging to an inferior race, unworthy to touch the holy things?

But do you realize?

Now and then you even forbid her to ascend to the altar, reverently to read to the assembly a text of Scripture. Any man goes first. All he has to do is be a man.

Does this not seem to you to be exaggerating things?

Are you still the slaves of ancient cultures, in which a woman was of no account, in which she was subjugated by male arrogance and destined only to live behind a curtain like the women of the Muslims?

One would say that you have no prophecy, that you have no truth to proclaim. Above all one would say that you are still living in the past.

---

*In *I, Francis*, Carretto assumes the voice of St. Francis of Assisi to address the Church and the world of the saint's time, as well as our own.

The past is past and does not return.

It has taken two thousand years for the gospel to begin to enter the hard necks of men who are externally Christian but who are stuck back in the circumcision. But now something is breaking through.

The Council has been a singular milestone in the transformation of the modern world, sweeping away a dead weight that burdened the Church.

And it could be this because, after so much suffering, the gospel had penetrated to the very tips of its veins.

The political concept of the ancient theocratic state, in which we ourselves lived in the Middle Ages, where faith and culture, faith and politics, were one, is definitively superseded in the maturity of the gospel, especially in these times of yours.

The juridicism of the ancients is submerged by the charity that conquers hearts.

The unconfessed racisms of caste have been reduced to dust by the sense of quality announced and effectuated by the building of the kingdom.

There is something new for women, too. Read carefully.

Today a woman must hear the words of Jesus as a man hears them; and if Jesus says, "Go and make disciples of all nations," it must no longer be that a man hears this in one way and a woman in another.

How you must rethink everything! And how I would like to say to women of today, "Go!" with all the force of which my spirit is capable, and all my anxiety for the immense needs of a world athirst for the gospel. This is an urgent invitation.

Transform your home into a convent — an ideal, spiritual one, as St. Catherine did. Let prayer reign there, good counsel, and peace. Let your toil, wherever it is, be illumined by the power of your calling — for you were made to love, to comfort, to serve.

Do not copy men. Be authentic. Seek, in your femaleness, the root that distinguishes you from them. It is unmistakable, for it has been willed and created by God himself. Repeat to yourselves every day: A man is not a woman.

Waste no time in approaching men in order somehow to resemble them. Rather seek to remove yourselves as far as possible from their model. It is not yours, and it is rather marred and muddled even so.

I think there is a model for you women in the world. Mary of Nazareth.

It is scarcely possible that Jesus would not have thought of this during the thirty years of his earthly existence, or that he would not have sought to mold and shape a model for women.

Mary was so close to him!

And she was so attentive to him!

And she was altogether the Daughter of the Father, the Mother of the Word, the Spouse of the Spirit.

We have not yet sufficiently considered this exceptional woman. We have not plumbed the depths of her reality as "woman of this earth," as our sister. We have not sufficiently considered her freedom, her autonomy, her self-fulfillment, day-by-day in her everyday life. You women are going to have to be the ones to dig out something of the mystery of Mary, in prayer.

There has been too much sentimentality, and too much useless triumphalism! Especially coming from men. Especially if they are not married.

And one more thing. Do not let yourselves be guided by men any longer just because they are men. If you let them lead you do so because they are saints and do not disdain the help of persons like Clare — who, though she is a woman, can tell you things of utility and power. — *I, Francis*

THE CHURCH IN MINIATURE

Thanks to the merciful goodness of our God, I have devoted practically my entire life to proclaiming the gospel. On every continent where I have been privileged to go and meet my brothers and sisters in the faith, I have seen amazing things.

And I keep seeing more.

And especially I see a new thing, filling me with joy: the Christian home becoming more and more *the Church in miniature.*

When I used to go to church as a boy, religious practice was essentially centered on "the priest."

The laity I knew, patronizingly described as *vulgus indoctus,* were still immature and inert, a flock of sheep, with a cleric on whose shoulders fell the full weight of the apostolate.

Then came a new age.

Beginning in the pontificate of Pius XI and increasingly through the reigns of Pius XII, John XXIII, and Paul VI a process of development took place on a vast scale within the Church.

The laity became aware of forming the Church and grasped the fact that their faith didn't merely urge them to acts of piety but required them to live out the gospel message in the world.

Everything became the material of religion: home, politics, social relations, job, life, love.

The Second Vatican Council — the most extraordinary religious event to have taken place in all the centuries of Christianity — effected the Church's transit from childhood to maturity, obliging everyone to see the Church as the *people of God* and no longer as a clerical pyramid.

This achievement was of enormous significance and in fact formed the theological basis for the new concept of Church-and-world. Even though we haven't yet achieved in entirety what the new perspectives, afforded by the Council, may reveal, we have made a great deal of progress.

Without the presence of the laity and without a just, fruitful, balanced, loving collaboration between hierarchy and laity, the life, the activity of a Christian community, whether large or small, would be inconceivable today.

This is maturity!

This is the conscious response to the wealth of prophetic content in God's word, *"You are a people of priests"* (1 Pet. 2:9).

Yes, a people of priests, not people bossed by a priest.

The priestly task — that of living the life of Jesus in his absolute self-giving to the Father and of offering all earthly reality to the Father — is now the responsibility of all the baptized, in the unity of the Holy Spirit.

What may we not expect to see in the Church, once this becomes a complete, mature, genuine fact?

There certainly won't be anymore crises over lack of vocations, since from now on all vocations will be priestly!

No longer shall we have a Church expressing itself exclusively in terms of "rite" and "public worship," but a Church acting and making itself felt as the leaven in the dough, as the salt of the earth.

My readers will forgive me for having wanted once again to break a lance on behalf of my favorite topic: the presence of the laity in the Church.

It's because once again, now as my death draws near, I've had the joy of experiencing the beauty of brotherly love, of the genuine apostolate, that came to me through the vision of *the family as the Church in miniature.*

I had fallen ill . . . seriously enough to feel the total weakness of someone overpowered by pain and by days full of bitterness and poverty.

In this condition I was gathered up by a Christian family who carried me off to their house in the mountains, to see — which was more than kind of them — whether there was any chance of getting me better.

For two months I was treated with prodigious hospitality by Christians not only determined to make me strong again but eager to pray together and live together in an atmosphere of love and spiritual joy.

There, while thinking about myself and what had happened to me, the idea came to me that I ought to encourage all those people who feel alone or without support in their lives to break out of their loneliness and try and live the Project "Church," meaning community, charity, prayer, through friendship and sharing.

"Woe to him who is alone," says the Scripture (Eccles. 5:10), and how true this is!

And how true it is that we ought, while there is yet time, to commit ourselves with all our strength to holding the front-door open to the spreading of the gospel, to praying in common, and to the wonders of forming the Church.

Then we shall find we aren't alone anymore and friends will be like children begotten in our youth, "sharp arrows in the quiver," who will help us, as Psalm 127 says, "when the enemy comes to parley at the gate."

— *And God Saw That It Was Good*

5

A Brother to All

BACK TO THE WORLD

The first time I stayed for any length of time in the desert, and acquired a taste for it, I experienced the profound longing to stay there forever, which is not surprising!

A superficial acquaintance with the world one is leaving behind is enough to convince one that not much will be lost by abandoning the city and (somewhat more difficult) its inhabitants.

The deep peace I enjoyed during the long, healing silences, the delight of the clean, luminous horizons of the Sahara, the pleasure of the solitude, and, better still, the face-to-face encounter with God were gifts that outmatched anything my youthful dreams had given me, or the heavy demands made on me by my involvement as a human being in the earthly city.

And yet, underlying this human longing to hide among the dunes and live in a small desert *tsar* among poor and simple people, was a certain uneasiness of conscience. Do you want to remain in the desert because you like it, or in order to seek God?

Do you love the desert because you no longer love men? Are you trying to stay here because the idea of going back there is distasteful to you? "If so, go back," said my conscience. "If so, go back," said my superior. I remember one conversation I had with the man who at that time, in the name of God and of the Church, was acting as my spiritual director. "Carlo, during these years of solitude you have discovered God as the Absolute and you have fallen in love with him. But now you must discover another absolute: human beings. Before, perhaps, when you spoke of working for the apostolate, you were doing so under the impulse of nature. Now you must do it under the impulse of grace. Originally, perhaps, you enjoyed it; now you must do it because it costs you something. And remember one important truth, which made of Père de Foucauld one of the prophets of our time: one must live out the life of contemplation among one's fellow human beings. And if you want one phrase that sums up his thought on the subject, remember this: 'Present to God and present to men.' " And so I found myself back in the world, in the midst of all the confusions, surrounded by my fellow men and women.

Things had changed, however, and above all my vision of humanity had changed. Humanity too is an absolute, I would repeat to myself each time someone came to visit me in the fraternity, distracting me from my prayer.

But does prayer simply mean remaining on one's knees? That could be so convenient in times of stress.

And then I realized in a new way that even prayer can become an escape. Yes, an escape from reality when that reality is charity, love....

Humanity too is an absolute, and you must seek, love, and serve human beings just as you seek, love, and serve God. Jesus left us in no doubt about this inexorable and simultaneous movement into the two dimensions, the horizontal and the vertical.

The closer you come to God as you ascend the slopes of contemplation, the greater grows your craving to love human beings on the level of action. The perfection of men and women on earth consists in the integration, vital and authentic, of our love for God and our love for human beings.

It is quite useless to look for convenient escape routes: there are none, because Jesus himself welded together into one single commandment the two elements that humans, in their apathy, only too frequently separate: "You must love the Lord your God with all your heart, and your neighbor as yourself."

And since, with our skill in casuistry, we found it easy to separate what he had joined, he established another with the authority of his blood, shed to the last drop: "I give you a new commandment: love one another just as I have loved you."

After that, anyone who wants to go on arguing can do so, but he should not then delude himself that he is a close friend of Christ. To separate our love of God from love of our fellow men and women is a fundamental betrayal of the gospel ideal.

To take to one's prayers when the village is burning and the inhabitants crying for help is to create an untenable excuse for one's own laziness and one's own fear.

That is why a Church that concentrates on its own ritual and is not aware of the sufferings and anxieties of human beings, of the chains that bind them, is a dead Church, with nothing more to say about the heart and mind of its founder.

That is why the scandal of piety based on processions, Masses for the dead, and private devotional practices unrelated to the evangelization of the poor gets swept to one side by the protest of those who still believe in the inexorable power of the word of God.   — *In Search of the Beyond*

THE LAST PLACE

I became a Little Brother of Jesus because God called me. I never doubted the call. Equally, if God hadn't called me I couldn't have survived for long!

Sleeping in the open, living in rough climates, associating with really poor tribes and putting up with the stench: all this is small compared with the revolution in one's personality, the breaking off with the past, the living among civilizations and peoples so different from one's own.

As you know, the Little Brother may not have a life apart. He must choose a village, a slum, a nomadic town, settle in it, and live as all the others live, especially as the poorest live....

Here is the secret of the wide acceptance of Charles de Foucauld. He arrived, undefended, among savage tribesmen like the Tuareg. He came to the Arab world dressed as an Arab. He lived among those who were the servants of the Europeans as though they were his masters. He built his hermitages, not on Roman or Gothic lines, but on the simplicity and poverty of the Saharan mosques.

Being poor, dressing like "them," accepting their language and customs, he immediately knocked down the barriers and lived in dialogue with them. Real dialogue: between equals.

I shall never forget a scene that, in its simplicity, expresses concretely the degree of love in this new "going toward them who do not yet know Christ." I was traveling by camel along the track between Géryville and El Abiodh, heading for a desert area to spend some days in solitude.

At a certain point along the track I came to a work detail. About fifty natives, under the direction of a minor official of the Engineer Corps, were toiling to repair the road, ruined by the winter rain.

No machines, no technology under the Saharan sun; only the toil of wielding the shovel and pick all day in the heat and the dust. I passed up the line of workmen scattered on the track, replying to their greetings and offering the liters of water in my *gherba* for their thirst.

At a certain point, among the mouths approaching the *gherba* to drink, I saw a smile break out which I shall never forget.

Poor, ragged, sweating, dirty: it was Brother Paul, a Little Brother who had chosen that detail in which to live out his Calvary, to be a kind of leaven there.

Nobody would have detected the European underneath those clothes, that beard and that turban, yellow from the dust and the sun. I knew Brother Paul well, because we had been novices together.

A Parisian engineer, he had been working on the Reganna atomic bomb when he heard the Lord's call.

He left everything and became a Little Brother. Now he was there. Nobody knew he was an engineer. He was a poor man like the others.

I remember his mother when she came to the novitiate on the occasion of his making his vows.

"Brother Charles," she had said, "help me understand my son's vocation! I have made him an engineer; you have made him a manual laborer. Why? You might at least have used my son for what he is worth! Wouldn't it be more advantageous, more useful for the Church to have him work as an intellectual?"

"There are things," I replied, "we cannot understand by mere intellect and common sense. Only faith can enlighten us. Why did Jesus wish to be poor? Why did he wish to hide his divinity and power and live among us as the least of us? Why the defeat of the cross, the scandal of Calvary, the ignominy of death for him who was life? No, the Church doesn't need one more engineer; she needs a grain of wheat to die in her furrows."

So many things cannot be understood on this earth. Isn't everything around us a mystery?

I can understand why Paul had to give up everything — his way of life, his career — for love of God and love of his brethren. But I also understood the reactions of his mother. Indeed, many would say: "What a pity! Such an intelligent person going to work in the Sahara! He could have built a printing press for making available good literature. He could have...." And they would be right, too.

It's difficult to fathom the mystery of humanity, which is part of the great mystery of God. There are those who dream of a powerful Church, rich in resources and potential, and there are those who want her poor and weak. There are those who devote their lives to study in order to enrich Christian thought, and those who renounce study for love of God and their neighbor. That is the mystery of faith!

Paul was not interested in having influence upon human beings. He was content to pray, to disappear. Others will search other paths and achieve holiness in other ways. Can I doubt the faith of my mother, who would have desired all riches to be in the hands of the Church, to be used for more effective missions?

And I, her son, quite the opposite: dreaming of a simpler faith, a more deeply felt poverty, and above all a vocation founded on the lack of riches. Wasn't I right in a way, too?

It's so difficult to judge! So difficult that Jesus besought us not to try to answer these questions.

But to one truth we must always cling desperately — to love!

It is love which justifies our actions; love must initiate all we do. Love is the fulfillment of the law.

If, out of love, Brother Paul has chosen to die on a desert track, by this he is justified.

If, out of love, Don Bosco and Mother Seton built schools and hospitals, by this they were justified.

If, out of love, Thomas Aquinas spent his life among books, by this he was justified.

The only problem is to put into their right perspective these different kinds of "love-in-action." And here Jesus himself teaches us in an uncompromising way: "The greatest among you must be as the least, the leader be as one who is a servant."

And again: "A man can have no greater love than to lay down his life for his friends."   — *Letters from the Desert*

GOD IN CREATION

People are already worrying about the time, now not far off, when our mechanical civilization can offer everyone not just one day off a week but two or even three. What shall we do with so much free time?

Congress follows congress, and apocalyptic voices are raised in warning as if we had reached the world's end — when not knowing what to do men and woman will go mad or at least collapse into a state of nervous exhaustion. I hope only that among the multitudes of pagans who add to their cars a private yacht or plane there will still be some Christians capable of occupying their spare time in working for others. Nothing to do? Then I suggest you take a look at the outskirts of our cities.

That is where the refuse of life's great sea ends up, even in our prosperous consumer states. It is difficult to know where to begin, there is so much to be done, so many wounds to soothe.

Where do ex-prisoners go? How do ex-prostitutes live? Where are the rivers of subnormal people hidden? Have you ever visited mental hospitals, old folks' homes?

Have you never gone into the slums? Or into deserted country hamlets where only the old peasants are left, most of them incapable of work in the fields? Time on your hands?

Have you never thought, out of love for Christ, of spending a day, just a day, with an old peasant to help him cut his corn on the hillside because he cannot afford a mechanical mower? Time on your hands?

Has it never occurred to you to spend a day in the dirtiest house in some village helping the poor woman straighten up a bit and giving her a chance to catch her breath?

What is that in comparison with the ocean of evils washing over humanity? Nothing, practically nothing. But it is an act of love like Jesus' death on Calvary, and an act of love can achieve a lot. If nothing else, it can give you a bit of true peace and the world the impression that hope is still possible.

Not much?

I think it is. . . .

If only our hearts were always tender and our souls fresh when we look at creation! What a source of joy it would be on our pilgrimage!

We can pass by and see, or we can pass by and not see: it depends on us.

Creation is like a message written on things, a story told in symbol, a source of conversation for our souls.

But we have to learn how to read, listen, and converse.

We are in constant danger of our hearts turning to stone, either with old age or with the petrifaction of sin: and then it is goodbye to our hymn, goodbye to our conversation!

We become the deaf mutes of the Gospel, and in that case, only Jesus can cure us.

Loving nature, conversing with nature, is not something extraneous to our love for God: it is a part of it, an essential ingredient.

God speaks to us, teaches us, gives us his first revelation, in the symbols of the created world. Later we shall receive the revelation in word and later still a direct, personal revelation from God, but things still continue to reveal God, as God himself intended, and we cannot forget it.

Not to look at nature, not to love it to the full, is to refuse to read a document God has specifically composed for us in his love.

St. Francis thoroughly understood this truth and made it his own, very particularly his own, and he managed to write that masterpiece of love, the *Canticle of Creatures:* "My Lord be blessed for all his creatures."

There is more, however, much more, and it is perhaps our own time which is discovering it. The universe is not only a means whereby God reveals himself to us, a sort of document in which the Creator explains things to us, but a reality that contains him. I can even say that it is a kind of Host concealing God himself under a mysterious veil.

God is *immanent* in his creatures, he is immense, he is everywhere.

I used to think this was only a catechism answer. But now I feel it for myself, much more deeply, much more intensely.

God is in nature, God is in matter: matter is divinized, vivified, by God's presence.

Now that I know these things I no longer kick stones about as I used to as a child; I have a greater understanding of the Asians who wish never to do violence to nature because they respect it too much as mediating God's presence.

Perhaps the medievals' love of and attachment to the divine Transcendence has helped us forget that God is also immanent, that he is everywhere. It has created in the past a Western religious concept that takes little or no account of natural realities, sees no connection between God and plants, between God and the animals around us.

I shall never forget a group of schoolboys waiting at a station in May sunshine throwing stones at the lizards and throwing the lizards with a laugh on the fire. Such things are relics of a time when a supposed love of God saw no connection with a love of nature and created people, even religious, who saw nothing wrong with hunting, and by that I mean not catching a hare or pheasant for the family to eat, but the brutal joy of seeing game twitch under the shower of lead.

These times have gone, but they are still a very recent thing.

— *Love Is for Living*

SAINTHOOD — JUST A DREAM?

At least once in our lives we have dreamed of becoming saints, of being saints.

Stumbling under the weight of the contradictions of our lives, for a fleeting moment we glimpsed the possibility of building within ourselves a place of simplicity and light.

Horrified at our own selfishness, we burst asunder the chains of the senses, at least in our desire, and glimpsed the possibility of true freedom and authentic love.

Bored by a middle-class, conformist life, we suddenly saw ourselves out on the streets of the world — bearers of a message of light and love, love of all sisters and brothers, and ready to offer, on the altar of unconditional love, the witness of a life in which the primacy of poverty and love would make communicating and relating an easy matter.

This is when Francis entered our lives in some way.

It would not be easy to find a Christian — Catholic, Protestant, or Orthodox — who has never identified the notion of human holiness with the figure of Francis of Assisi and who has not in some measure desired to imitate him.

As Jesus is the basis and ground of everything, as Mary is the mother par excellence, as Paul is the Apostle of the Gentiles — so Francis, in all Churches, is the incarnation, the ideal figure, of the human being who sets out on the adventure of sainthood and expresses it in a way that is truly universal. Anyone who has ever considered holiness possible in a human being has seen it in the poverty and tenderness of Francis, has joined himself or herself to the prayer of the Canticle of Creatures, has dreamed of going beyond the limits imposed on us by unbelief, the limits of fear, beyond which one should indeed be able to tame wolves and speak to the fishes and the swallows.

I think Francis of Assisi is in the depths of every human being, for all are touched by grace — just as the call to holiness is in the depths of every human being.

And yet at any moment in history, Francis, while profoundly incarnate in history, can be placed outside history as well.

He can be placed with the first Christians, who, as itinerants in the streets of the Roman Empire, bore with them the joy of a message that was really new. He can be placed among the medieval reformers, as the rebuilder of a Church enfeebled by political struggle and threatened by false compromise. He can be placed in the baroque era, challenging, with his strange poverty and humility, the pride of the clerical class, whose priesthood was that of lords of the people instead of as their

servants. He can be placed in the world of today as the prototype of the modern man or woman, sallying forth from anguish
and isolation to renew the discourse with nature, with human
beings, and with God.

Especially with God....

Here I am up in the Cave of Narni to spend a few months
in solitude.

Once more I have yielded to the temptation of the desert,
which has always been the love niche where I can encounter
the Absolute that is God, and the place where truth bursts out
in blossom. The Franciscan solitude of this lofty grotto rivals
the dunes of Béni-Abbès, or the harsh desert of Assekrem. At
bottom they all spring from the same root; for when Père de
Foucauld sought the African desert he was doing what Francis
had done when he sought the silence of the Subasio dungeons,
or the rough country of Sasso Spica at La Verna.

What counts is God, and the silence of an environment where
God is near.

I sought out this hermitage because it is one of the special
places of the Franciscan world, where the Saint sojourned on
repeated occasions, and where all blends together in a perfect
oneness. Forests, bare rock, the architecture, poverty, humility,
simplicity, and beauty, all go together to form one of the masterpieces of the Franciscan spirit — an example to the centuries of
peace, prayer, silence, ecology, beauty, and the human victory
over the contradictions of time.

When we behold these hermitages, abodes of men and women
of peace and prayer and joyous acceptance of poverty, we have the
answer to the anguished conflicts that torment our civilization.

You see, these rocks say to us, you see, peace is possible.
Do not seek for luxury when you build your houses, seek
the essentials. Poverty will become beauty then, and liberating
harmony — as you can see in this hermitage. Do not destroy
forests in order to build factories that swell the ranks of the unemployed and create unrest; help human beings to return to the

countryside, to learn again to appreciate a truly well-turned object, to feel the joy of silence and of contact with earth and sky. Do not hoard up money — inflation and greedy people lie in ambush for you; instead, leave the door of your heart open for a dialogue with your brother or sister, for service to the very poor.

Do not prostitute your labor fabricating things that last half a season, consuming what little raw material you have left; but make pails like the one you see here at this well — it has been drawing its water for centuries and is still in use.

The ill you speak of consumerism is a cover. You fill your mouth with words in order to stifle a bad conscience. Even as you speak, you are consumerism's slaves, without any capacity for innovation and imagination.

And then...

Unburden yourselves of your fear of your brothers and sisters! Go out to meet them unarmed and meek. They are human beings too, just like you, and they need love and trust, even as you.

Do not be concerned with "what you are to eat and with what you are to drink" (Matt. 6:25); be calm, and you shall lack nothing. "Set your hearts on his kingdom first, and on his righteousness" (Matt. 6:33), and everything else will be given to you for good measure. "Each day has enough trouble of its own" (Matt. 6:34).

Yes, this hermitage speaks. It speaks and says brotherly and sisterly love is possible.

It speaks and says that God is our Father, that creatures are our brothers and sisters, and that peace is joy.

All you have to do is will it.

Try it, brothers and sisters, try it, and you will see that it is possible. The gospel is true.

Jesus is the Son of God, and saves humankind.

Nonviolence is more constructive than violence.

Chastity is more pleasurable than impurity. Poverty is more exciting than wealth.

Try to think about it, sisters and brothers. What an extraordinary adventure lies here before us.

If we put Francis's project into execution we shall be escaping the atomic apocalypse.

Is it not always this way? God proposes peace.

Why not try it? — *I, Francis*

THE PRIMACY OF NONVIOLENCE

When I, Francis, happen to read the things which you have written of me since my death — so abundantly, and, I admit, in such good taste — I have to confess that what I like best is the account in the *Little Flowers.*

I feel comfortable there.

Sometimes it happens that I no longer recall whether the things recounted actually went that way, or instead are a bit exaggerated — or just plain made up? — but that has no importance.

I like them.

Even if they did not happen just that way, they are beautiful and good as told that way. I accept them all, for they give a photograph of me which, even if retouched by your generosity, is the photograph of nonviolence, a picture which I am honored to accept, and I thank you for having understood me.

For yes, that is what I was, nonviolent. And the *Little Flowers* are a beautiful dream for you and for me.

Deep within us, every one of us, are dreams of such a world, made peaceful with love and the sweetness of humility.

Is this not so? . . .

I have asked you not to speak overmuch of poverty today. Your environment is too ambiguous in its regard, and it is too difficult to explain your position in your bourgeois and socialist milieu. Instead, I tell you this, and I tell you most emphatically: Speak of nonviolence, be apostles of nonviolence, become nonviolent.

Now is the hour to do so, in fact it may be the last hour, in as much as you are all sitting on top of a stockpile of bombs, and you can blow up at any moment now.

Do not underestimate the danger. I have a strong feeling that you will have to suffer a thing or two before the end of the world.

It would be better to be prepared. And it would be still better to hope for the conversion of humanity.

Even Nineveh was converted, and saved.

Listen.

Today, when you talk nonviolence, everyone understands what you are talking about. It is a discourse that is clear and simple, and with its dynamic you can change the face of the earth.

You speak a great deal about human rights today, and this is good. Now, the first human right is not to be subjected to violence, to be left in peace.

This human right is one which is biblical in scope, and you should live it to the hilt.

But it is even broader than that. Much broader, in fact.

Nonviolence regards first of all nature, the skies, the seas, the mines, the forests, the air, water, the home.

These are the first objects of nonviolence. It is a terrible sin you have committed all around you, and I do not know whether or not you can still be saved.

You have violated the forests, defiled the seas, plundered everything like a bunch of bandits.

Your contempt for nature knows no bounds.

If there were a court of the skies, or of the seas, or of mines, you would all of you (or almost all) be under sentence of death.

And perhaps there is such a court. An invisible one. For your punishment has certainly begun.

You can scarcely breathe your air. Your food has become unhealthy.

Cancer assaults you with more and more regularity.

And now that you have destroyed nearly everything you have appointed me patron saint of ecology. You have to admit it is a little late.

I do not know what I shall be able to do.

The pity is that it is always the same ones who govern: the powerful, the rich, the professional politicians.

Try the little ones in the government — the simple, the poets! But who believes poets?

Try being governed by those who can still look at the stars at night, or spend an hour watching a beetle under a dry leaf in the forest, or dream over a glowworm in a field of May wheat.

These are the ones who would see humanity's problems better. At least they would not commit such horrors.

You have reached the point of no return. And you have no reason to complain: it is you who have been irresponsible.

You continue to manufacture machinery that exhausts your raw material and huge amounts of capital; and yet you do not offer the slightest assistance to the people who work the farms, where the world's real wealth is, and which are going to rack and ruin.

You turn out graduates only to enroll them in the ranks of the unemployed, and they become weary and mistrustful in your cities. You fail to seek to form young people who love constructive, simple toil, the toil of the artisan or of the farmer, young people who care more for a well-turned object or a loaf of whole-grain bread than they do for money.

If you need proof that you are off on the wrong track, consider well your sorrow. . . .

Your basic mistake is that you place money instead of truth and love at the top of your scale of values. After all, it is for money that you plunder nature, without the slightest thought that your errors will fall back upon your heads — as they are already doing.

But once done, a bad deed cannot be undone.

It would be more practical to cast a forward glance — knowing, however, that the conversion of human beings is not an easy matter.

Jeremiah said, "The human heart is incurable."

In your position, not being an economist, perhaps I would follow the intuition of an amateur, without making five-year plans, and look only at the welfare of persons and of the world of nature.

I would start by giving the primacy to the countryside. I would consider cities the first mistake.

Why do the cities of Italy, of Brazil, and so on, present the horrible spectacle of human beings heaped up in matchbox slums and living in such inhuman fashion?

Because governments do nothing for rural areas, and the human beings who live there, afraid of being left helpless and abandoned, flee in the hope of bettering their situation.

If governments gave minimal aid to the people who live in the country, and sought to make their life a human one, most of them would stay to cultivate the land — which of course is ultimately what sustains all of you, even those of you who live in the city.

This recent era of your history has seen the exodus from the countryside. The era of nonviolence, of which I dream, should see an exodus from the cities, and a massive return to the country.

Country people ought to be helped to live even if they only keep the trees alive or clean the irrigation ditches. For they shall thereby be defending the land against destruction and neglect.

Make the land a garden, and the garden will become an Eden, and will give you what you seek: bread and peace.

If a youngster sells a motorbike to buy a bicycle, give him or her a reward. If a farm manages to get its electric power from a windmill, or by burning waste, see that this is given public praise.

If upstanding industrialists begin raising cattle, or sowing their estates with spices, tell them thanks and knight them!

And another thing.

Litterers should be arrested. And fine anyone cutting down a tree without absolute necessity.

A boy or girl who tramples a flower or torments a lizard should have to go to bed without any supper; and the politicians who destroyed the olive trees in the plain of Gioia Taura should be removed from office.

Ah, but I see I am only reciting more legends, à la the *Little Flowers,* and that some of you are beginning to smile again. You do not believe me.

Well, I am a dreamer.

I am Francis of Assisi.

— I, Francis

CHILDREN OF THE SAME GOD

This evening Abdaraman is accompanying me to the hermitage for adoration. We walk the two hundred yards together, hand in hand and chatting. Abdaraman is a Muslim boy of perhaps eight years old. I say "perhaps" because no registry of births exists among his people; a child's birth is simply not recorded. So few people know their exact age.

Abdaraman does not go to school, even though there is one beyond the river, attended by the Europeans and some "Mozabites," the sons of local tradesmen. He doesn't go to school because his father Aleck won't let him go.

"Aleck," I asked him, "why don't you send your sons to school?" Aleck looked at me deeply. "Brother Charles, I don't send my sons to school because they become bad. Look at the boys who go to school. They don't pray, they no longer obey, and they care about nothing but the way they dress...."

The sun has set and the air has freshened. It is good to walk.
Abdaraman and I always have many things to talk about because we are really fond of one another. Every morning I find
him outside my cell waiting for me to finish my meditation.
Often we have tea together and he tells me how much he likes
the bread I make. Abdaraman is always hungry. But he never
asks me for anything; it is always I who have to guess that he
wants food.

This evening he is serious, and answers my questions with
difficulty. I realize that he has something important to say to
me and hesitates to do so.

But I know it won't be long before he speaks, because there
are no secrets between him and me.

"What's the matter, Abdaraman?"

Silence.

"Are you hungry?"

Silence.

"Did Daddy spank you?"

Silence.

"Has your bird escaped from its cage?"

Silence.

"Speak to me, Abdaraman. You know I am your friend."
Abdaraman bursts into tears, his body shaking. Tears stream
down his face and then continue down onto his chest and
abdomen.

Now it's my turn to be silent. I must await the stilling of
the storm.

I squeeze his hands harder as a sign of affection.

"Well, then, Abdaraman, what's making you cry?"

"Brother Charles, I am crying because you don't become a
Muslim!"

"Oh," I exclaim, "and why should I become a Muslim?
Abdaraman, I am a Christian and believe in Jesus. I believe in
the God who created heaven and earth, just as you do, and
our prayers go to the same heaven, because there's only one

God. It is he who has created us, who feeds us and loves us. If you do your duty, don't rob, don't kill, don't tell lies, and follow the voice of your conscience, then you'll go to heaven, and it'll be the same heaven as mine, if I too have done what God commanded me. Don't cry anymore."

"No, no," Abdaraman cries. "If you don't become a Muslim you'll go to hell like all Christians!"

"Oh, what a thought, Abdaraman! Who told you I would go to hell if I didn't become a Muslim?"

"A man in the village told me that all Christians go to hell. And I don't want you to go to hell."

We have almost reached the hermitage, and Abdaraman stops. He has never come any further than this. He has always stopped ten steps away from that building, and he would not enter for all the gold in the world, as though inside there were some mysterious deviltry forbidden to little Muslims. His love for me, and it is great, has always been injured by this wall which divides us and which this evening is taking on such an absolutely terrible name — hell.

I tell him, "No, Abdaraman. God is good and will save both of us. He will save your father, too, and we shall all go to heaven. Don't believe that just because I am a Christian I shall go to hell, as I don't believe you'll go there just because you're a Muslim. God is so good! Perhaps you didn't understand really what the man meant. Perhaps he said that bad Christians go to hell. Cheer up! Go home and say your prayers while I say mine. And before you finish, say this to God and I'll say it too: 'Lord, let all men and women be saved!' Go on...." And sadly I entered the hermitage, this little mud building, constructed by the same Charles de Foucauld who wanted to be called the Little Brother of all, and who was murdered, through ignorance and fanaticism, by sons of the same tribe as Aleck and Abdaraman.

But this evening it is difficult for me to pray. What a tumult of thoughts my little friend has aroused in me!

Poor little Abdaraman! You, too, are a victim of fanaticism, the stormy zeal of religious people, the so-called "men of God," who would send half the human race to hell, just because they are not "one of us." How can the thread of love that links me to a brother be broken by an alleged purity of faith, or that religion, instead of being a bridge of union, should become a trench of death, or at least of unconfessed hate? We're best off without it, this religion which divided us. Best to fumble around in the dark than to possess a light like that!

After an hour's effort to face my poor soul with the silence of the Eucharist, I realized that tears were staining my white robe. I was the one to weep now.

While examining my conscience in order to cleanse my soul, not Abdaraman's, from sectarianism, a scene from my childhood rose again to my mind. I was eight years old then, the same age as Abdaraman. I lived in a village in the shade of an ancient church tower. The townspeople were not very religious, but they were excessively narrow-minded in their "purity of faith."

One day a man came to sell books, going from house to house. I didn't understand much then, but it was the first time I understood the word Bible. An unusual commotion seized the village. First the women, then everybody. Some out of zeal, some out of human respect. The excitement quickly reached the children.

The hysterical cry of a woman shouting from a window: "Rascal! You rascal! We don't need your religion. Go away!"

The man was walking in the middle of the street. His books were in a big, heavy bag.

A woman from behind him threw a book she had bought a few minutes before.

Without turning around, the man bent down to pick it up. A stone from a boy hit him in the back. The man quickened his pace, followed at some distance by the boys, each carrying a stone. I was among them. That evening at May Devotions the parish priest praised us for defending the parish citadel.

At a distance of forty years, and particularly this evening, that event acquired a new meaning for me.

I had never confessed to throwing a stone at an undefended man, out of religious zeal at that. The episode is recorded in a world that used to accept things of that kind, without seeing all their heinousness.

Nearly half a century later things have changed. There is something new in the air. A breath from the Spirit is animating the whole universe. An old world is dying, and a new one is being born. New concerns, new needs, new forces. We are at the dawn of an epoch marked by a great desire, at least, for love and peace among peoples and nations. Truth and charity are again striving to meet one another; respect for the individual is increasingly championed among all peoples.

An ecumenical spirit is loosening the most complicated knots, and the desire to know one another is far greater than the temptation to remain closed in the old citadel of our presumed truth.

Human beings, perhaps for the first time, are going into the field undefended, hopeful of fruitful encounters, of making friends of strangers.

Abdaraman, my dear little Abdaraman, have no fear: we shall love one another again, and we shall meet one another — and not only in heaven. *— Letters from the Desert*

6

Prayer

TIME FOR PRAYER

"You shall love the Lord your God with all your heart, with all your soul, with all your strength, and with all your mind; and your neighbor as yourself." (Luke 10:27)

In our day, as soon as you speak about the mystery of prayer, people cry, "Prayer! There is no time for prayer! All those people to feed, all those real things to organize, how can you still ask us to waste our precious time?

"Why search for a hypothetical relationship with the invisible God when you can find the immediate and concrete in visible human beings?

"And persons are the visible presence of God on earth: serve them, save them, and you've done it all!"

And what can we say when this stand is taken not least by the witnesses of the invisible God, by priests and religious? "Brother Carlo, you are speaking of the desert, of silence, of prayer.

"But how can you talk like that to us, when we are up to our necks in contemporary civilization, snowed under by thousands and thousands of tasks, caught up from morning to night in contacts with men and women and the service of the poor? And you keep silence with a compassionate smile and with the security of a person who continues to believe firmly in past prejudices."

But the fact is that they are not past prejudices!

The fact is that the priest who says he no longer has time to pray will be found on a painful search for his identity after a few years. The busy activists who have so little time that they can't waste time praying will be found so empty in a few years that you won't know what to do to give them back a little faith in the ideal they have been wanting to serve until now.

No, these are not prejudices.

The first commandment remains the first commandment, and it is the *first* — both under the old law (see Deut. 6:5) and under the new (see Luke 12:30) that was pronounced by Jesus — "You shall love the Lord your God with all your heart, with all your soul, with all your strength, and with all your mind; and your neighbor as yourself" (Luke 10:27).

Moreover, it is hammered in so forcefully that it leaves no doubts. It would seem that no part of the person has been forgotten on the list — heart, soul, mind, strength in order to emphasize the necessity of decision in loving God!

And then?

And then the problem. If you don't pray, if you are not searching for a personal relationship with God, if you don't stay with God for long periods in order to know, study, and understand him, little by little you will start forgetting, your memory will weaken, you will no longer recognize him. You will not be able to, because you will no longer know how to love.

The proverb "Out of sight out of mind" is true not only about persons; it is terribly true about God, too.

Take an example. If a man telephones his fiancée to tell her, "I'm sorry, this evening I can't come, I've so much work!," there is nothing wrong. But if it is the thousandth time he has made the same call, he has not been to see her in weeks on the excuse of work or outings with his friends, it is more serious — rather, it is quite clear: this is not love.

Because the lover is capable of overcoming all difficulties and discovering all the stratagems necessary to meet his soul's beloved.

So it is better to get clear with ourselves what our relationship with God is.

Have you been not praying, not seeking God personally because you don't love God, or because you have no time?

Usually we are afraid to accept the first reality; it is easier to fix on the second.

This is the true problem, which we do not try to resolve because our minds are confused....

Now I should like to say a word to anyone who has the heart of an activist, who has always had the impression that to pray is to run the risk of alienation from our brothers and sisters and their troubles.

This point of view is not completely wrong, I know. In the past too many people gave the impression of a Christianity that was otherworldly, absent. Today's thirst is for concreteness and reality, I know. But listen to this simple, linear testimony:

Here in Béni-Abbès, during the winter, nomads often arrive with their tents.

They are the poorest of men: they no longer have any camels or goats to sell, no longer the strength to organize caravans. They are seeking some place they can be helped to settle down into a new social reality that has no further need for the nomadic life.

One day a French woman, who was making a retreat here, was walking beside one of these tents. She stopped to pass the time of day and, as she did so, realized that a Tuareg girl, thin as a rake, was trembling with cold.

It is strange, but that is how it is: in the desert it is cold in the sunless dawns.

"Why don't you cover yourself up?" she asked.

"Because I've nothing to cover myself with," replied the girl.

The French woman, without going to the roots of the problem, went to pray.

She entered the hermitage built by Père de Foucauld himself, where the Blessed Sacrament is exposed.

She prostrated herself in the sand before Jesus, present under the sign of faith, "the Eucharist."

Some time passed, she sought contact with the Eternal One, she tried to pray.

"I couldn't go on," she told me afterward. "I couldn't pray. I had to go out, back to the tent, and give that child one of my sweaters. Then I returned, and then I was able to pray."

Here is what I should like to say to those who are afraid of personal prayer with God, who don't want to alienate themselves from their suffering brothers and sisters.

If you pray, if you pray seriously, if you pray in truth, it will be God himself who will send you out, with greater strength, with greater love, toward your brothers and sisters, so that you may love them more gratuitously and serve them more delicately.

Well, then, you will say, why, why in the past have too many Christians scandalized me with their indifference, with the hardness of their bigoted hearts, with the hermetic sealing of themselves against every problem of justice and liberation of the people?

Yet they were praying, they were contemplating!

No, if they were praying, their prayer was just a bit of rhetoric. If they were contemplating, they were contemplating... nothing.

They were deceiving you, and they were deceiving the Church.

It is impossible to pray to a personal God — that is, love a personal God — and remain indifferent to your suffering brothers and sisters. It is impossible.

Anyone who prays without suffering for one's suffering brothers and sisters is praying to a pole, a shadow, not to the living God.

Because if you pray to the living God, you who are living, God, the Living One, sends you to your living brothers and sisters.

If you pray to the living God, your prayer passes through the heart of Christ Crucified, the only model of the way we must love God and our brothers and sisters, the point of convergence between the vertical dimension of the Absolute and the horizontal dimension of all humanity needing salvation.

After Christ it is no longer possible to separate the love of God from the love of our brothers and sisters.

If you begin by loving your brothers and sisters, keep well in mind that you cannot separate this love from love for God.

God is a person — with a right to be loved, just as your brothers and sisters have a right to be loved.

And persons are loved for themselves, not for other ends.

To love others and use them for other ends is, in poor words, to exploit them, and today everybody agrees that this must not happen.

And if we agree not to exploit other persons, why should we end by exploiting God? So you cannot say "By loving my brothers and sisters I love God," just as you cannot say "By loving God, I love my brothers and sisters."

You must love God, and you must love your brothers and sisters, every one of them.

Love is personal, and it is strong and tenacious only if it is personal.

You cannot say "I love Christ present in the assembly of the faithful," if you do not first love Christ in himself as a person.

It is certain that the mystical Christ, which is the Church, is to be loved in his mysterious presence in the people of God, but there also exists the person of Christ, who must be loved passionately.

There also exists the person of the Holy Spirit who must be loved personally with all your strength, with all your heart, with all your self.

And that is what the first commandment means.

— *The God Who Comes*

SOMETHING MISSING

I've done a lot of work for the Church — I'm aware of it. It has been my only thought, my only care. I have raced hard and covered as many miles as the most committed missionary. At a certain point it occurred to me that what the Church lacked was not work, activity, the building of projects, or a commitment to bring in souls. What was missing, *or at least was scarce, was the element of prayer, meditation, self-giving, intimacy with God, fidelity to the Holy Spirit and the conviction that he was the real builder of the Church:* in a word, the supernatural element. Let me make myself clear: people of action are needed in the Church but we have to be very careful that their *action does not smother the more delicate but much more important element of prayer.*

If action is missing and there is prayer, the Church lives on, it keeps on breathing, but if prayer is missing and there is only action, the Church withers and dies. Let me give you a physical example from the desert under my nose (the desert is a great teacher!). Imagine a stretch of desert which is all dead sand, at most a few thorns. People decide to transform this desert into a blooming oasis. They set to work. They build roads, side streets, canals, bridges, houses, etc., etc. Nothing changes: it's all *still desert.* The basic element is missing: water. Now anyone who had understood this (it's strange how well we understand the physical world and how little we understand the supernatural) would begin work not *on the surface* but would set about digging deep. They would look for water. They would dig a well. The fertility of an oasis does not depend on the construction of canals, roads, or houses, but on that well. If water springs up everything will have life, if not *nihil.*

The fact is that Jesus told us, "Without me, nihil." It is this that I saw in Europe. A crazy army of Catholics is building away at houses, colleges, associations, and parties and almost nobody is bothering to dig wells. The result: sadness, discouragement, internal emptiness, and sometimes desperation. They are trying to build for God without God.

And don't tell me, sister, that they are praying. No, they're not praying, even if they say a hundred rosaries a day, even if they go to Mass regularly. *Prayer is something quite different!* Prayer is adoration of God and his will, not a jumble of formulae created for the very purpose of smothering the soul and shutting it into the tentacles of habit and the ready-made. Prayer is breathing, love, freedom, inexhaustible dialogue, and above all it is *thinking about God.* This is what is missing from our old-style Christianity, which when it wants to pray starts trotting out formulae. Look at priests. If they prayed seriously, when they came to talk to us they would tell us new things about that God who is *always new,* and instead they tell us the same old things and we go out from their preaching without any fervor.

Real prayer — and we have to be mature to understand this — is the silent adoration of God. You put yourself in front of the Blessed Sacrament which is here on Earth just to teach us to pray, and starting from him — the bridge between the human and the divine — you reach the Father in the thrust of the Spirit. One hour a day, at least, of this sunshine cure gets into the swing of that real prayer which is the starting point for heaven. Once our faith becomes lively and strong, then our *being Christian* takes on new flavor and is not just heated-up soup.

I am convinced that if Catholic Action, the militant Congregations and the priests, in short the backbone of the Church, gave *half* its energies to prayer, it would achieve much better results. This is why I left Rome; now I've told you plainly: I too was one of those crazy people, working furiously and not praying sufficiently.

Now I have understood, and I want to aim straight at the heart of God: the rest no longer matters to me, or at least it matters only if it enters into God's plan.

— Letters to Dolcidia

PRAYER FROM THE HEART

When I left for the desert I left everything behind me as Jesus had asked me to — I left family, house, money, situation. The only thing I didn't leave were my ideas about God, which were all packed into a big book about theology, and this book I took with me.

And there on the sand I went on reading and rereading this book as if God were contained in an idea and as if I could communicate with God because I had fine ideas about him.

My novice master said to me, "Brother Carlo, leave those books alone. Put yourself stripped and humble in front of the Eucharist. Empty yourself, de-intellectualize yourself, try to love, try to contemplate...." But I didn't understand a word of what he was trying to say to me. I remained thoroughly anchored to my ideas.

So he thought it would help me to empty myself, and to understand, if he sent me to work.

My goodness!

It isn't easy to work in those oases in the heat of the day!

When I returned to the fraternity I felt absolutely whacked, all my strength drained out of me.

I collapsed onto the matting in front of the Sacrament in the chapel, my head aching, my back breaking. And all my ideas flew away like birds flying from an open cage.

I couldn't even start to pray. I was arid, empty, exhausted. The only thing that came from my mouth was a groan.

The only positive thing that I felt, and that I began to understand, was solidarity with the poor, the truly poor, with anyone crushed under the weight of the daily yoke, with anyone on the assembly line. And I thought of my mother praying with five children around her feet, and of the peasants who had to work a twelve-hour day in the summer.

If peace and quiet were a prerequisite of prayer, then those poor people wouldn't have ever been able to pray. So evidently the prayer I had abundantly practiced up till then was the prayer of the rich, the prayer of comfortable, well-fed people who were masters of their own timetable.

I no longer understood anything, or rather I was beginning to understand a great deal.

I wept!

My tears fell on the coveralls that were a mark of my poor man's toil. And it was in that state of authentic poverty that I made the most important discovery of my life of prayer.

Do you want to know what it was?

That prayer takes place in the heart, not in the head.

I felt as if a vein were opening in my heart and for the first time I "experienced" a new dimension of the union with God.

What an extraordinary adventure I was embarking on.

I shall never forget that moment.

I was like an olive crushed in the press.

Yet over and above the oppression, it was unspeakably sweet to feel the reality in which I was living sweeping over me.

I was in total peace. The pain accepted in love was like a gateway enabling me to pass beyond mere things.

I intuited the stability of God. Since that time I have always thought that that was contemplative prayer.

The gift that God makes of himself to those who offer their lives, as the Gospel says: "Whosoever loses his life for my sake will find it" (Matt. 10:39).   — *The Desert in the City*

•

St. Peter's Day

God, my *Creator!* Source and root of my being, I love you. I seek you. You are everything to me.

Now that I am tainted by sin, re-create me, renew me, take me back to your creative embrace, and give me back the aspect you envisaged for me when you made me.

Life-giving air, water for those dying of thirst and bread for the hungry are as nothing, compared with what you are to me.

You are the arms in which I have my existence, the root on which I stand, the Whole on which I depend. I am yours, make me yours; I am in you, gather me closer to you. Remember what your Spirit said in Zechariah: "made beautiful with my beauty" (9:17). All the rest is mine, but unfortunately the only thing left is sin. God, I love you. *— The Desert Journal*

PIERCING THE CLOUD

Those persons whose contemplation is their life do not need many words to pray.

They need one word, at the most two...I am not trying to make some sort of joke: their one word of prayer will be enough to sum up everything they wish to say once their whole life, in its deepest intimacy, has been transformed into prayer.

Let me explain.

Because our prayer on earth is a tension between God's greatness and our smallness, between the abyss of the Absolute and the abyss of our nothingness, between the incommunicability of the divine Transcendence and the possessed irrationality of sin, we feel the need to cast our prayer up like a flaming arrow toward the divine Mystery or down into the abyss of sin, the expression of our deepest wretchedness.

We therefore feel urged both to cry our thirst for the Almighty with a word which is the name of God and to remind ourselves of the state of our soul, which is "sin."

We need only these two words, which we forge into steel darts that seek to pierce the Cloud of God's Unknowing, thereby expressing all the insatiability of our prayer.

God, Sin, the English mystics used to say.

Kyrie eleison, pomiliu Ciospodz, say the Greeks and Russians in the long litanies so typical of their liturgy.

The Latins more often express this drama of love in other ways: *Jesus, I love you, have mercy on me.*

And it is certainly magnificent to remain there, one's whole soul poised between those two phrases, with no other wish than to throw oneself toward the Cloud of Unknowing and pierce it with the sheer force of one's love; than to throw oneself toward the Cloud which conceals God in his naked Being and which the soul seeks in the darkness of faith without considering itself and without distractions from external things.

Nothing can be more profitable than this loving effort on the soul's part sharpened to one word of prayer.

Nothing is more useful for the persons concerned and their loved ones, for the living and dead, for the whole Church.

Nothing is more definitive for people during their earthly pilgrimage, nothing better sums up their "contemplation on the road."

The person who has reached this position needs only to continue without deviating to right or left, knowing that "what is to come must come thence."

When St. Thomas, at the completion of his work on the *Summa,* had a momentary experience in prayer of God's Transcendence concealed in the Cloud of Unknowing, he cried out in ecstasy: "Everything I have written is but straw."

Not that straw is useless, and well he knew it!

Without it, without the long stem, how can the ear on top reach up to open itself to the action of God's sun?

Theology, culture, philosophy, science are the human stem slowly bearing the ear of our soul toward the warmth of the divine sun.

But once the ear lies in the sun and begins to open with the approach of autumn, the stem becomes straw because its work is finished and the soul needs nothing but sun before being harvested into God's eternal granary.   — *Love Is for Living*

AND THE NIGHT SHALL BE
CLEAR AS THE DAY

I got up at three o'clock to pray.

Very quietly, so as not to wake the brethren, who were sleeping in the adjoining cells, I went out into the night.

I crossed the courtyard, and found myself in complete darkness. There was a cold nip in the air, but I was sufficiently protected by my *burnous*.

I left the hermitage buildings behind me, and made for the nearby slope in order to watch the stars.

This, for me, is the best preparation for prayer.

Above my head, in all its magnificence, stretched the winter sky of Béni-Abbès.

The profound darkness resulting from the absence of the moon, which was in its last quarter, made it particularly easy to see the stars. . . .

I always count it as something precious when, before embarking on my prayer, I am able to fill my gaze with the pure, mysterious light that comes from the stars. . . .

People really make me laugh when they say, "You have to bring everything into your prayer, every aspect of yourself." It is obvious that they are talking about prayer in the abstract, as one might talk about the polar icecap without ever having seen it, or about journeying across the desert when one has never so much as set eyes on a sand dune. Bring everything? I can tell you I would like to bring nothing with me, to contrive, for an hour at least, to forget myself, my poor head, and my heart. To succeed in keeping my imagination in check, bundling it into some corner or other in order to be left in peace, just for that one hour.

And then there are those who come and tell you, with impressive arguments, that you must bring your fellow men and women with you, have them present continually.

"My God!" a receptionist once said to me, "from morning till night I'm harassed by my neighbors, first at home, then in the office, and then in the course of my various social engagements. When can I find five minutes to be alone with God?" The receptionist was right, and not those who ramble on about prayer without ever having had any real experience of it. In order to pray, one needs a modicum of solitude, of detachment and withdrawal. This is what the desert, retreat, getting down on one's knees, is all about. One cannot spend all one's time with the community; otherwise one ends up denying that God is the Absolute. Do not be alarmed. I shall return to my brethren, of course I shall. Jesus himself compels me to do so, though I assure you that, were it not for him, I would flee to the desert and never come back.

To all community enthusiasts I say: all right, I will give you twenty-three hours, but allow me to have the twenty-fourth alone with God.

To take prayer seriously means giving at least the twenty-fourth hour to God — and to God alone.

Simply because he is God, the Absolute.

He is entitled to expect that I should drop everything for him, just as the visitor who comes to see me has the right to expect it. . . .

Here and only here, in fact, is to be found the meaning of prayer, the power that sustains it, and the hope that gives it life: there is one who seeks you, one who stands before you saying: "Look, I am standing at the door, knocking. If one of you hears me calling and opens the door, I will come and share his meal, side by side with him" (Rev. 3:20). If prayer meant addressing oneself to a mute, unheeding wall, I guarantee the Bible would never have been written. I guarantee that the saints would have grown wise to the fact, and years ago the abbey of Monte Cassino, the monasteries of Mount Athos or in the Tibetan mountains would have fallen into ruin.

Prayer is meaningful because in your presence Another is present, another mouth corresponds to your mouth, another ear to your ear.

In this way it becomes something real, vital, authentic.

Under the impulse of this conviction I managed to get up in the night — and I can tell you it is not pleasant.

And it is filled with this hope that I now prepare myself for prayer. I go back down the slope and reenter the hermitage. It is the same one that Père de Foucauld, thirsting for prayer, built for himself in this desert of Béni-Abbès.

The room, poor as any other, with walls of beaten clay and earthen floor, covered by a layer of beautiful clean sand from the dunes, is of an extreme simplicity.

The bright flame of the sanctuary lamp, fed by the purest olive oil, flickers and casts its light into the semi-darkness.

I wrap my soul round with that light, and my body with the *burnous* which keeps me warm, and kneel down on the sand to pray.

You will ask me: why did you go back inside?

Could you not pray under the stars? Would it not have been easier? Is not nature the principal reminder we have of Almighty God?

And you might even be right, but you must listen to my explanation. There is no absolute law about praying in church. One can find God perfectly well out under the stars, or in the midst of the city crowds. We have all tried these things out ourselves. But...

There are three really important things in my life: the Cosmos, the Bible, and the Eucharist.

I could pray outside under the stars, which represent the Cosmos for me; I could pray with the Bible, which is the Word of God; but if I can I prefer to pray before the Eucharist, which is the very presence of him for whom everything was created and who was revealed by the Bible as savior of the world.

The Eucharist recapitulates the Cosmos for me; the Eucharist recapitulates the Bible for me. All three bear the divine within them, and all three are worthy to be there while I am praying, but the third is the greatest....

When, in the desert, my novice master left me alone for eight days; when, later on, I remained alone in a hermitage for forty days, I would have gone mad had it not been for this presence answering to the needs of my presence, this love responding to the demands of my love.

It is here that I felt the presence of God most strongly; it is here that I have experienced for myself Christ's dramatic recapitulation of the history of salvation.

And I always come back here when I want to make my way to the threshold of the invisible, because the Eucharist is the surest doorway opening onto it.

Here I am, then, alone before that door — or, rather, that window which opens onto the invisible at the extreme limits of human reality. Faith alone is my guide, and I assure you that I know both in my heart and in my flesh what "mystery of faith" means.

To find oneself confronted by a piece of bread, and to believe that it is the presence of Jesus, involves an act of faith: reason is inadequate.

But faith is bare, dark and frequently painful.

Once I get past the barrier of my feelings, however, and cast myself with confidence into the abyss of God, my faith is joined by hope, and love sustains me. Just as each of the three Divine Persons seeks the other two within the framework of the unity, so each of the theological virtues gathers to itself the other two theological virtues. And as soon as you succeed in holding them strongly within your grasp, keeping them united before you, you can fashion a sword sharp enough to cut through to the invisible.

The sign of bread both conceals and points to the presence of Jesus; faith, hope, and charity cut through the barrier that separates me from him and reveal his presence. It is Jesus himself, Son of God and son of Mary, Jesus of Bethlehem, of Nazareth, of the Last Supper, of Calvary, Jesus of the resurrection, yesterday, today, and the same forever.

— In Search of the Beyond

THE GOD OF THE IMPOSSIBLE

An accident in the middle of the desert paralyzed one of my legs. When the doctor arrived — eight days later — it was too late; I shall be lame for the rest of my life.

Stretched out on a mat in the cell of an old Saharan fort, I looked at the marks made by time on the mud wall, whitewashed in lime by the soldiers of the Foreign Legion. The heat made it difficult to think. I preferred to pray. But there are certain moments when prayer is not easy.

I remained silent, trying mentally to take my soul beyond the compounds of my room into the little Arab-style chapel where I knew the Eucharist was. The brothers were working some distance away, some in the fields, some in the workshop. My leg was hurting terribly, and I had to work up the force to stop my mind wandering. I remembered Pius XII once asking in one of his audiences, "What does Jesus do in the Eucharist?" and he awaited the reply from us students. Even today, after so many years, I do not know how to reply.

What does Jesus do in the Eucharist? I have thought about it often. In the Eucharist Jesus is immobilized not in one leg only, but both, and in his hands as well. He is reduced to a little piece of white bread. The world needs him so much and yet he doesn't speak. Men and women need him so much and he doesn't move!

The Eucharist is the silence of God, the weakness of God.

To reduce himself to bread while the world is so noisy, so agitated, so confused.

It is as though the world and the Eucharist were walking in opposite directions. And they seem to get further and further from one another.

One has to be courageous not to let oneself be carried along by the world's march; one needs faith and will power to go cross-current toward the Eucharist, to stop, to be silent, to worship. And one needs really strong faith to understand the impotence and defeat which the Eucharist represents and which is today what the impotence and defeat of Calvary was yesterday.

And yet this powerless Jesus, nailed down and annihilated, is the God of the Impossible, Alpha and Omega, the beginning and the end....

Jesus is God of the Impossible; my powerlessness shows his power; my insignificance as a creature shows his being as the creator.

From Job, in his struggle with his creator, God asked an act of trust, by pointing to the magnificence of creation.

> Where were you when I laid the earth's foundations? Who decided the dimensions of it, do you know? Or who stretched the measuring line across it? What supports its pillars at their bases? Who laid its cornerstone when all the stars of the morning were singing with joy? (Job 38:4–7)

Today, a saying of Jesus' in the Gospel impresses me more than this quotation about the power of the creator and the absolute powerlessness of the creature: "It is easier for a camel to pass through the eye of a needle than for a rich man to enter the kingdom of heaven" (Matt. 19:23).

This expression comes to my mind every time I see a camel on the track, and it makes me smile. If he had said "A horse or an ox ... " but no, a camel, with a hump! Of course a camel can't be made to pass through the eye of a needle!

To create the firmament is certainly a sign of great power, but to make a camel pass through the eye of a needle seems to me greater still; it's quite impossible.

In fact, to the worried and amazed apostles who exclaimed, "Then it is impossible to be saved," Jesus calmly replied, "What is impossible for man is possible for God."

"For you all things are possible," Jesus was to say to the Father in the prayer of Gethsemane. Omnipotence is an attribute of God's.

The real qualities of my humanity are insignificance, weakness, misery, powerlessness. There must be a meaning to this. One must think about it carefully. Is it possible that sin, which invaded the world soon after the creation of human beings and which seems at times so inexplicable, has nothing to tell us about God's omnipotence?

Is it possible that the human weakness we see in old age, sickness and death should be something which simply afflicts us and has no further meaning?

When I think of my evening examinations of conscience, it is always a question of things not done or done badly; I can never list positive things.

And even if I can achieve inner peace for a moment, I still have a deep sense of my inadequacy and wretchedness, and I have to admit my incapacity to make my love greater.

My awareness of being unable to make an act of perfect love keeps returning to my mind.

I have experienced the same thing in prayer. Left to myself, with my own strength, I have felt the painful reality that without God's help we cannot say even "Abba, Father."

There are moments when God makes us feel the extreme limits of our powerlessness; then, and only then, do we understand our nothingness right down to the depths.

For so many years, for too many years, I have fought against my powerlessness, my weakness. Often I have refused to admit it to myself, preferring to appear in public with a nice mask of self-assurance.

It is pride that will not let us admit this powerlessness; pride that won't let us accept being inadequate. God has made me understand this, little by little.

Now I don't fight anymore; I try to accept myself. I try to face up to myself without illusions, dreams or fantasies. It's a step forward, I believe. And if I had made the step while I was still learning the catechism I should have gained forty years.

Now I contrast my powerlessness with the powerfulness of God, the heap of my sins with the completeness of God's mercy, and I place the abyss of my smallness beneath the abyss of his greatness.

I seem now to have reached a means of encountering him in a way I have never known before: a togetherness I had never experienced before, an awareness of his love I had never previously felt. Yes, it is really my misery which attracts his power, my wounds which shout after him, my nothingness which makes him throw himself open to me.

And this meeting between God's totality and human nothingness is the greatest wonder of creation. It is the most beautiful betrothal because its bond is a love that gives itself freely and a love that accepts. Really, it is the truth of God and humanity. The acceptance of this truth comes from humility, and that is why without humility there is no truth, and without truth no humility.

"He has regarded the lowliness of his handmaiden," said Mary when she saw, accepting her nothingness, the essential love of God and felt her flesh become the dwelling place and nourishment of the Word Incarnate.

How wonderful that Mary's nothingness should attract God's all. What sweetness in her prayer when she recognized that she was at the opposite pole from God, where humility not only becomes the acceptance of love, but is one of its demands.

What peace in her total self-giving to him, accompanied by the contemplative gaze at the greatness and perfection of the beloved.

No more perfect relationship exists, and Mary shows in its most perfect form the absorbent thirst of the soul under God's dew.

Thus, after so many years, I feel I have found the solution to the only real problem we have on earth. I have recognized my powerlessness, and this was grace. In faith, hope, and love I have contemplated the all-powerfulness of God and this, too, was grace.

God can do everything and I can do nothing. But if I offer this nothing in prayer to God, everything becomes possible in me.

I remember the great rock where I was weighed down by my self-centeredness, closed in my purgatory for having denied Kada the blanket.

Within myself I feel the inability to perform an act of perfect love, following Jesus on Calvary, dying with him on the Cross.

Thousands and thousands of years may pass and my position will not change. But... but what is impossible for me, the rich man in the Gospel, is possible for God! It is he who will give me the grace to transform myself; he will make me able to carry out the impossible and remove the obstacle which separated me from the kingdom. And so it is a question of waiting, of humble and trustful prayer, of patience and hope. But the God of the Impossible won't ignore my cry.   — *Letters from the Desert*

•

Come, Holy Spirit,
send us from heaven
a ray of your light.
Come, father of the poor,
come, bestower of gifts,
come, light of our hearts.

You are the perfect consoler,
sweet guest of the soul,
most gentle refreshment.
You are repose in our toil,
coolness in our heat,
comfort in our tears.
O most blessed light,
invade our hearts,
for without your strength,
there is nothing in us.
Wash what is soiled,
bathe what is parched,
heal what is bleeding,
bend what is rigid,
melt what is frozen,
straighten what is crooked.
Give to your faithful
who trust in you alone
your holy gifts.
Give virtue and rewards,
give us a holy death,
give us eternal joy.
Amen.

       — *The Desert in the City*

7

Last Things

DO WITH ME WHAT YOU WILL

I think about death.
I try to see it as life, as wood needed for the fire
as a field in which a treasure is hidden
as a book to be opened
as seed which has to flower
as a secret which I have to know
as a *crossing* which I have to make.

The word applying most accurately to death is really the last one: "crossing."

This was typified by the Hebrews' crossing of the Red Sea, and actualized by Christ's "crossing" through his own Exodus on the night of the resurrection.

It is the instant which precedes the light.

It is the state of waiting.

It is faith in God the Creator.

It is hope placed in the God of the Impossible.

It is the love required before you can really possess love. The one who has explained all this and made it so is Jesus.

Jesus the first-born Son.

The first to rise from the dead.

And, having made the victorious crossing, having first paid the price, the one who turns to us and says, "Do not be afraid. I have overcome the world" (John 16:33).

What occurred on the night of the resurrection henceforth concerns us personally.

It was indeed the "crossing" of all humanity in Christ, head of the body that is the Church, and first of all the saved.

What occurred is so extraordinary that the Church seems to be mad with joy when she sings the Exultet.

And to see someone rise from the dead is enough to send anyone mad: life rekindling in the extinct ashes of human nature, the sudden blaze exploding from the darkness.

This means that God is God, that life goes on and that there is an explanation for all things, even those most baffling or apparently shocking.

It means that humanity is eternal and that death, which used to frighten us so much and painfully dominate our existence, is now explained, understood, taken captive, and conquered.

Now I can laugh, laugh too about my former fears.

Now that I have seen the Risen Christ, I can face my own death with the certainty — that I too shall rise again.

But let me try and extend the concept of death as "crossing" to what happens to us every day, every hour, every second of our spiritual and physical existence.

Generally we apply the word "death" merely to the moment when we expire, to the one that puts an end to our earthly existence. But the reality is deeper and more all-embracing; death is not, I think, only something concerned with the last day of our lives, but, as I was saying, with every day of our lives.

Every second of our existence, by its nature, contains a painful element of death and, at the same time, by virtue of Christ's resurrection, a true and explosive element of resurrection.

These two realities are hidden within us, just as Christ's death and resurrection are hidden within us.

> In our body we always carry the death of Jesus, so that in our body the life of Jesus may always be manifest too.
>
> (2 Cor. 4:10)

The conflict between the two realities is the crossing into the kingdom, that kingdom that Christ has already declared to be "present within us" (Luke 17:21) and which is developing and expanding until it reaches its completion at the end of the world.

It is the transition between the visible and the invisible, the frontier between human nature and divine nature, the fruit of every good desire, the value of every sacrifice, the ratification of every loving deed, the genuine slow gestation into children of the Father.

Yes, the duality "death-life," to which Christ's own death and resurrection have given seal and explanation, plenitude, and the promise of irruption into the kingdom, is unquestionably the key to all the whys and wherefores that torment us and the right answer to the objections raised in the human heart. Death and life, taken together and particularly when in conflict, signify the beginning of things, the perennial evolution of the creation, life's successive leaps forward, the splendid days of Genesis, God's way of going about begetting his son and passing on his own experience of love to him.

Our dying to earth is a progressive emergence from the womb of matter and history, so that we may gradually acquire the stability of the kingdom and full communication with God.

— *Summoned by Love*

THE FACE OF CRUCIFIED LOVE

What did Jesus do to conquer evil?
What did he do to destroy death?
What is the meaning of these two expressions:
To conquer evil?
To destroy death?
How can we say this if, after Jesus, the world has gone on as before, sinning and dying?
Nothing has changed since Nazareth; nothing has changed since Calvary.

The world has gone on subsisting with its crimes and massacres; the human race has continued on its way with its slaveries and tears.

What has happened for us to be able to say, "Jesus has saved us"?

What has occurred to affirm that, after him, death was destroyed and evil conquered?

Yes, this is the problem and we have to approach it with clear heads if we are to understand and solve it.

By living the way he lived, Jesus conquered evil single-handed, and by dying the way he died, he swallowed up death.

The problem is personal rather than universal.

Jesus gave the example by living as he lived, by dying as he died; he explained to us how we should act in order to conquer evil and destroy death.

Human beings, do you want to free yourselves from the evil oppressing you?

Act as Jesus did.

Human beings, do you want to destroy death, which is ever clutching at you?

Die of love, as Jesus did.

To overcome the evil seeking to master us, to transform our death into an act of love, is to achieve that conquest necessary for entering the kingdom, I mean the kingdom of peace and freedom, the kingdom of justice and love.

No one can discharge this task for us.

It's true, Jesus has saved us, but he's left the hard work of saving ourselves to us.

His death has justified us all, he being the Son of God, but he hasn't brought us bodily into the kingdom; he has asked us to follow him.

Since Jesus' sacrifice, each one of us is safe, but we each have to work out our own salvation.

In this resides the dignity of the human creature: being a child in relation to the Father.

In this resides the dignity of human suffering.

In this resides freedom.

Since Jesus died of love, each of us ought to die of love.

— And God Saw That It Was Good

•

To accept death as an act of love is not easy, and I believe that this was the climax of Christ's achievement in his travail toward love.

And it is for us to imitate him, even in our weakness.

But death, real death, is not physical death; this is only the outward sign of it, the horrible visible palpable representation of it.

Real death is separation from God, and this is unbearable; real death is faithlessness, hopelessness, lovelessness.

We all know what pain and sadness are, for we have all experienced them and are all immersed in them.

Real death is the chaos where human beings find themselves when they disobey the Father, it is the tangled web to which they are reduced by their passions, it is the total defeat of all their dreams of greatness, it is the disintegration of their whole personality.

Real death is emptiness, darkness, desolation, despair, hatred, destruction.

So ... Christ agreed to enter into this death, into this separation, so as to identify himself with all who were in separation, and to save them.

When he had touched the depths of their despair he announced hope with his resurrection.

When he was immersed in their darkness he made the brightness of truth burst forth with his resurrection.

When engulfed in the abyss of their lovelessness he showed them the infinite joy of love with his resurrection. By rising from the dead Christ made all things new.

By rising from the dead he opened new heavens.

By rising from the dead he opened new life.

— Blessed Are You Who Believed

THE FIRE OF CHARITY

If the Master should knock on my door tonight and tell me that my earthly pilgrimage is at an end, I feel that on balance I should not be consigned to hell.

Why?

Because neither God nor myself wishes it, he for love of me, I for love of him. Despite immense evil in me, I feel, in the strength of his love, the desire to be with him, and this seems to me to be quite normal between friends. I know sin as ignorance and even more so as weakness, but I have never felt "opposed" to God. I cannot even visualize — thanks to his grace — the "sin against the Holy Spirit"; I cannot imagine how someone could impugn the known truth. Theologians discuss it at length, but their subtleties do not impress me.

I was saying, then, that if I died today, I should not on balance be condemned to an eternity of torment. But then neither should I be admitted to heaven! I am not ready for it. I felt that very, very keenly under the rock when I had denied Kada my blanket, and I still feel it today, Good Friday, as I meditate on our Lord's passion. Yes, I am afraid to suffer for others; I tremble before the cold blade of charity.

And so? If I am not to go to hell and heaven is too good for me, where shall I go?

I must stay here, I cannot pass beyond, and purgatory is certainly this side of the eternal watershed.

I am not a theologian, but even theologians know little about purgatory. It is a passing place or state or condition in which those not yet ready for the kingdom of Perfect Love pray and suffer and so prepare themselves for the day when they will be admitted to the eternal banquet.

I imagine purgatory to be like the large cupboard where my grandmother put medlars to ripen. Please forgive this curious comparison. When I was young, I occasionally stayed at my grandmother's house, which was a farm in the Langhe hills of Piedmont, and I remember my grandmother putting the medlars that were still not ripe by the autumn into this cupboard, among the straw. "Everything comes to him who waits." A spiritual fruit that has failed to ripen under the sun of God's charity will ripen in the cupboard.

The comparison is perhaps a good one because the cupboard is part of the house.

I should not like to offend anyone's sensibilities, and so I say this from a purely personal point of view, but I think of purgatory as being this side of eternity and therefore still tied to my home. I think of the souls of the dead completing their period of expiation near where they lived, perhaps even in their homes themselves. If I can make a request at the moment of death, I know what I shall ask: "Send me to the stretch of desert between Tit and Silet," where I had the deepest insight into the need for perfect love at the earliest possible moment.

And the fire? Ah, I thought that question would come.

Well, I think there is fire but not of a material kind. Many times as a boy, especially in the sacristies of mountain churches, I have seen the souls in purgatory wrapped in flames — real flames with fiery tongues higher than the highest heads there. It is natural for artists to think and paint in this way: how else could one depict the spiritual fire of purgatory? In the Middle Ages, and since, the flames are always shown as real ones, simply because it is easier that way.

Everyone, however, knows that real fire would damage the body...and the body is not in purgatory but in the cemetery, like a piece of cast-off clothing.

To touch my soul another type of fire is necessary: charity, which I rejected on earth, or at least did not fully accept. Now that I have my back to the wall, I cannot escape it any longer, I must accept it. I cannot put it off any more.

The fire of charity, that is, this supernatural kind of love, will attack my soul as flames attack wood. My soul will writhe, sizzle, and smoke like green wood, but it will burn in the end. Not a single fiber shall escape; all must be consumed by that divine love.

How long will this take? It will go on until the work is done. Some people will need no more than a few days, others thousands of years; the important thing is that the purification must be completed. All this will take place while a sort of film of our lives is screened before our eyes.

There is more than enough there. When I think that I shall have to relive in slow motion certain episodes in my life which I did not subject to the flames of love but constructed on egoism, falsehood, cowardice, and pride, and all the time with the fire of charity in my veins, I can assure you that it comes home to me what a serious, deadly serious, business it will be. Imagine me arriving in purgatory wearing a mask put together with years of patience and skill which I have never dared or been able to remove for fear of revealing myself as I really am to God and human beings.

When the fire of love licks up at it, gets beneath it, and burns it off my soul, it will, I have no doubt, prove an agonizing experience. And what will happen when the fire starts to burn the property to which I was clinging so firmly: a blanket perhaps, or a piece of meat I took first from the plate when Jesus would have wanted me to be last?

No there is no need for a coal fire to burn my soul: the fire of failed responsibility, of injustices, of thefts, of lies, of help denied to someone who needed me, of love not lived with those who were my brothers and sisters, is more than sufficient.

Not very much, you say? Well, that is only a part of it, the part we can imagine by the standards of earthly justice. True justice, measured on God's justice, on the Transcendence of the Absolute, appalled St. John of the Cross when he was undergoing the terrors of the dark night of the soul.

Yes, the fire of purgatory is charity, that is, the highest degree of love in its supernatural state.

It is the fire that consumed Jesus' sacrifice on Calvary, the fire that burned the saints with inextinguishable love, the fire that led the martyrs to martyrdom and baptized them if they were not already baptized, giving them access to the kingdom. We shall not escape this fire; nothing we do can avert it.

On the other hand I should not wish to escape it. I know it will hurt, but I also know that I have to go through it.

I have no desire to continue for all eternity the ups and downs of my sensibility, the perennial resistance to the fire of love. I am green wood, and I do not wish to enter Paradise still green. I want to burn in purgatory and then be finished with it.

I want to go where Jesus went, to feel what he felt in his divine heart. I shall suffer, I know, but there is no other way, and in any case God's power will be there beside me to bring me assistance.

Here and now I accept that fire which will smelt from me and my earthly slag the hidden metal of my person, willed by God but obscured by sin.

I shall be given a new face, the face that God saw when he drew me from the primeval chaos and that Satan sullied with his slaver.

I shall emerge a child, God's child forever.

And since purgatory is this side of the eternal watershed, the only appropriate course for me is to combine it with my life on earth, pretend I am already there, apply the fire of charity to myself a little at a time but courageously, start to burn out the clinkers, at least the biggest and most obvious ones.

What I do here I shall not need to do hereafter: I have therefore gained. I must accept the asceticism my life imposes on me, the sufferings and trials I experience on the road, the tedium and troubles of human society, the inconveniences and inevitable illnesses as precious and providential opportunities for advance payment.

I say "opportunities," because there is more to paying than suffering. One must suffer with love, with patience, otherwise it is useless. We were saved not by the scourges on Jesus' flesh but by the love with which he accepted them.

We were redeemed not by his road to Calvary but by the patience, mercy, obedience with which he trod it.

In short, the Redemption renewed the world by Jesus' charity. Charity is the essence of Christianity. Yes, we can state with absolute certainty that *love is for living*.

And if we can transform every moment of our existence into an act of love, all our problems will be resolved. The fire of purgatory is love, and if we wish to avoid purgatory, we must accept its fire on earth.   — *Love Is for Living*

IT IS EASTER

Life and death [are] but two aspects of one and the same thing, as also sorrow and joy, light and darkness, cold and heat.

It [is] as if the real were cut in half by a door.

It was with good reason that Christ presented himself in this way: "I am the door."

The door is the same one on both sides.

The earth, the visible, the sensible, time, and space, are on this side; heaven, the invisible, the eternal, the infinite, are on the other side.

But everything is one, logical, and true.

The door that is Christ is Lord at once of the here and the beyond, as Christ is crucified here and glorious beyond.

To become immortal, to enter into the glory of the Risen Christ, every person must pass through this door, and the one who opens and closes it is the Lord. As Revelation says, "If I open, no one closes."

This passage is called Easter, and the first to make it was Christ the Lord — as it is said, "This is the Pasch of the Lord."

Everything on this side of the door has its meaning and can be understood only in function of, in the embrace of, what is beyond.

Short of this relationship, the succession of things here below cannot involve the real, and you use up your life without seeing.

Things in time without any reference to the eternal acquire no meaning. They are as nothing, like dried-up leaves. Jesus himself said: "Do not store up treasures for yourselves on earth, where moths and woodworms destroy them and thieves can break in and steal."

And he added, "But store up treasures for yourselves in heaven, where neither moth nor woodworms destroy and thieves cannot break in and steal" (Matt. 6:19–20).

The resurrection of Christ gives meaning and life to every creature, as created by the Father, and actualized in view of, and through, Jesus Christ.

And creatures, through him, have two faces: one crucified, here, and one glorious, beyond.

No person can escape this reality, and this is why the death of each one of us has a sorrowful face in reality and a glorious face in hope.

The passage is always a terrible trial, like coming to a boundless sea and then there is the explosion of joy as you watch the sea open.

So it was for the People of God, and so it is for us.

There is always the painful wait, and then a sudden light.

The wait is yours, the light is God's.

And it is gratuitous.

You can never claim you deserved it.

On the contrary!

No merit has the power to open the door.

It is only the gratuity of God's love that can manage this impassable lock.

"When he closes, nobody can open" (Rev. 3:7).

But his will is always prompt to open, for "I have come that they may have life and have it to the full" (John 10:10).

How often have you asked, "Why am I still here?"

And the reply is ever the same.

You must learn to love. For beyond the door there is nothing but love.   — I, Francis

THE RISK OF BELIEVING

It is useless to hide it. Faith is a trial, a tremendous trial, like death itself, and no one can get us out of it, not even God himself. . . .

Having faith means believing that he fills all space, that no leap can cast me out from his arms. Having faith means believing that he knows everything, that before I arrive he runs through the infinitely complicated plan of my existence all the way to its conclusion, like an ever new problem solved by his infinite love: my final entry into his kingdom.

Believing in God means all this and still more.

Only very late do we learn the price of the risk of believing, because only very late do we face up to the idea of death.

This is what is difficult: believing truly means dying. Dying to everything: to our reasoning, to our plans, to our past, to our childhood dreams, to our attachment to earth, and sometimes even to the sunlight, as at the moment of our physical death.

That is why faith is so difficult. It is so difficult to hear from Jesus a cry of anguish for us and our difficulties in believing, "Oh, if only you could believe!"

Because not even he can take our place in the leap of faith; it is up to us. It is like dying! It is up to us, and no one is able to take our place.

This mature act of faith is terribly, uniquely personal. Its risk involves us down to the core; the truest and greatest prototype of this act of faith that we, as the People of God, possess is the biblical account of the trial of Abraham. "God said, 'Take your son Isaac, your only one whom you love, and go to the land of Moriah. There you shall offer him up as a holocaust on a height that I will point out to you'" (Gen. 22:2). That is a leap of pure faith proposed to Abraham!

It is a personal act, and it is an act of death.

Without love it is impossible to understand such a proposal; on the contrary, it is scandalous.

But for anyone who loves?

Seeing God wrapped round the colossal figure of this patriarch, alone in the desert beside his tent . . . no, that is no scandal, but quite the contrary.

God wants to communicate with the depths of Abraham's being and tear him from himself and his involvement with his own problems, which are like self-centered possessions; He wants to make this creature of his "more his," this man who is destined not for the tents of earth, but for those of heaven. So God asks of him an absurd trial, as love is absurd for anyone who does not live it, but as true and relentless as love for anyone who possesses it. "Take your son . . . " (Gen. 22:2).

I believe that at dawn that morning the angels from every corner of heaven were busy preparing the mountain on which a man was about to carry out such a tragic and radical rite of love!

I believe that at sunrise on that eastern morning the space around Abraham was quilted by the invisible eyes of all those who had died before him, wanting to see what the ending would be!

What a drama was in the poor heart of that man! God had asked the supreme sacrifice. If Abraham had had to turn the knife on himself it would have been easier!

An act of pure faith is the death of what we love most so it may be offered to the loved one, because only love is stronger than death.

> Set me as a seal on your heart,
> as a seal on your arm;
> For stern as death is love....
> Deep waters cannot quench love,
> nor floods sweep it away.
> (Song of Songs 8:6–7)

No, the floods of thought and reasoning before the absurdity of the request, the floods of emotion before the affection of Isaac cannot quench in Abraham's heart the act of love that binds him to his God, his "beloved above everything," the apex of all values.

God is God, and Abraham runs the risk right to the end.

God is God and he takes up all rational space and also that which humanity thinks is irrational.

God is God, and he puts everything right in his love for his creature.

He will not permit him to come to harm in his act of loving God.

Faith is not separated from love and hope!

At the ultimate moment of trial, when we try to pierce the invisible with the sharpened spear of every possibility we can find, we realize that the three theological virtues — faith, hope, and charity — are really only one, and that they have such a power of penetration that they could disrupt the entire universe.

On Mount Moriah, in the trial of Abraham, humanity embraced God as never before. The experience of this embrace reverberates through the religious history of the world as an epic of a love greater than humanity's endless frailty.

Not for nothing does this tragic rite of love conclude with an extraordinary promise from God.

> "I swear by myself," declares the Lord, "that because you acted as you did in not withholding from me your beloved son, I will bless you abundantly and make your descendants as countless as the stars of the sky and the sands of the seashore; your descendants shall take possession of the gates of their enemies, and in your descendants all the nations of the earth shall find blessing — all this because you obeyed my command." (Gen. 22:16–18)

I do not know whether in my life I shall be presented with such a hard act of faith as Abraham was. I hope not, for I am small and weak.

But I know I shall be presented with one of the same kind: *my death*.

That is why I said the price of the risk of faith is death itself. It is personal. It is mine.

It makes me smile to hear the nonsense spoken by those who try to distract me from this real problem. It is I who have to die. And dying is a leap into the dark that I have to get used to little by little.

Every act of faith I make in my life is training for this hard passage. Reasoning certainly does not solve the problem. Neither does the thought that Christianity is an organ of social justice and the liberation of oppressed peoples. This distribution of my land to the poor, this freedom of peoples to which I have contributed with all my energy are only the beginning. They are the entrance visa to a more radical distribution and a more complete liberation that death imposes on me.

At the very moment of my death I must carry out an action that is terribly irrational for anyone who has seen only the earth, terribly painful for anyone still attached to it, terribly scandalous for anyone who believes so little in the Absolute as to remain grounded and petrified with fear.

But I hope it will not be so for me.

I hope not, because I cling onto faith as the only table of salvation.

I hope not, because as long as I have breath in me, night and day, I sharpen my weapons for the final agony.

I hope not, because I say every hour, "I do believe! Help my lack of trust!" (Mark 9:24).   — *The God Who Comes*

RISEN LIFE

When you see a forest ravaged by storms
and earthquakes blasting the land
and fire burning down your home
say to yourself: I believe
that the forest will come to life again
the land will be calm again
and I shall remake my home.

When you hear rumors of war and people everywhere are dying of terror, when "nation shall rise against nation and kingdom against kingdom" (Matt. 24:7), say bravely to yourself, "Jesus warned me of this and he added: 'Look up and raise your heads, because your redemption is drawing near' " (Luke 21:28).

When sin has you in its grip and you feel utterly defeated, say to yourself, "Christ is risen from the dead and I shall rise from my sin."

When old age or illness embitters your life, say, "Christ is risen from the dead and has made a new heaven and a new earth." When you see your son running away from home in search of adventure and your cherished dream as father or mother crumbles around you, say, "My son will not run away from God; he will come back because God loves him."

When charity seems to have vanished forever and you see others sunk in sin and drunk with treachery, say to yourself, "They will touch the depths but they will return because no one can live away from God."

When the world seems a defeat for God and you are sick with the disorder, the violence, the terror, the war on the streets; when the earth seems to be chaos, say to yourself, "Jesus died and rose again on purpose to save, and his salvation is already with us."

When your father or your mother, your son or your daughter, your spouse or your friend are on their deathbed, and you are looking at them in the pain of parting, say, "We shall see each other again in the kingdom. Courage."

This is what it means to believe in the resurrection.

But there is more.

Belief in the risen Christ means something else.

For Mother Teresa of Calcutta it means comforting the dying, and for you it means doing the same.

For Martin Luther King it meant facing death, and for you it means being unafraid to die for your brothers and sisters.

For Abbé Schultz, prior of Taizé, it means opening his convent to hope, and for you opening your house to hope.

Every departing missionary is an act of faith in the resurrection.

Every newly opened leper hospital is an act of faith in the resurrection.

Every peace treaty is an act of faith in the resurrection.

Every agreed commitment is an act of faith in the resurrection.

When you forgive your enemy
When you feed the hungry
When you defend the weak you believe in the resurrection.
When you have the courage to marry
When you welcome the newly born child
When you build your home

you believe in the resurrection.
When you wake at peace in the morning
When you sing to the rising sun
When you go to work with joy
you believe in the resurrection.

—*Blessed Are You Who Believed*

•

Come then, death!
Come, I am waiting.
You do not frighten me anymore.
I no longer see you as my foe.
I see you as a sister.
I look you in the face.
I understand you now.

And as you come toward me, I tell you, thinking of him who holds you firmly in his mighty hand, "Do with me what you will."

Wholeheartedly I say this to you. Truthfully I say this to you. Lovingly I say this to you:

"Do with me what you will."

Accustom me to this extreme abandonment.

Accustom me to this never-ending test,
to this never-adult kiss,
to this never-given change,
to this never-finished conversation.

Accustom me little by little, by distributing my death through all the days of my life.

Put it on my bread like ashes or sand, so that I do "not live by bread alone" (see Matt. 4:4).

Put it in my house as "something lacking," so that I do not accept the limitations of the visible.

Put it as insecurity into my security, so that I may only be secure in him who is the Absolute.

Put it as a reminder in the midst of my joys, so that I may grow used to being alone, as in that second when I shall be alone with you.

When my father was dying, he asked me to stay beside him. He had confidence in me and we were devoted to one another.

God granted me the grace to spend his last night at his bedside.

I sat beside him, holding his hand, and could tell from the way he squeezed mine what he wanted to say to me.

It was as though he wanted to lean on me, though he stared straight ahead.

Little by little, he grew more alone.

As he left the earth for the frontier of the invisible, he was alone.

No one could help him.

He was alone.

Yes, he did in fact die alone.

All help counts for nothing.

We are alone with God.

In the crossing, only God's hand can take you by the hand.

I took my hand away.

Only to God, at this point, can we say, "Do with me what you will," for he alone, being God, cannot disappoint our hope.

— *Summoned by Love*

FAREWELL

The time has come.

There is a passage in the Psalms that says: "Our life lasts for seventy years, eighty with good health..." (Ps. 90:10).

These words apply to me; I do not find them hard to accept.

I may also say that I don't want to go on much longer; even though I know that the gift of life is great, the gift of death is greater.

Do not be surprised at what I say. It may seem strange, but it is not. I have told you in every way I can think of that I believe in God and that I have committed my entire existence to this effort of belief.

Now, precisely in believing, I have come to a conclusion that I want to put as the endpiece to this book about my faith.

God has done great deeds. This is beyond doubt, and we are always saying so in our Church services: "His wisdom made the heavens, and the earth..." (see Ps. 136:5). And this is no small thing.

"He decides the number of the stars and gives each of them a name" (Ps. 147:4).

He made human beings, and wants them as his children.

He made the kingdom and destined us for it.

Well, among all those good and beautiful things, he has made one most beautiful of all. Death!

When you hear this for the first time, you may make a wry face or at least be very puzzled.

But there is no reason to be. Let me explain.

Go, some sunny day, to a nursing home, the place where children of refined sensibility today stockpile the elderly.

What does this place make you think of?

What do all those twisted limbs, extinguished eyes, and obvious sufferings suggest to you?

I know what they suggest to me: one thing —

"O blessed death, come, come, come, do not delay!"

I know. The most devout of you will say that even a single day of this life counts in completing what is lacking in the sufferings of Christ (see Col. 1:24). I know it, and I believe it, and accept everything that God decrees for me, from this time forward.

I know it!

But I am thinking about a different aspect, over which you cannot reproach me.

I have discovered, among all good and beautiful things God has made, that there is one no less beautiful, as I said, but even more beautiful — and that is death.

Why?

Because it enables me to start again. It enables me to see "new things."

Never as now have I understood so well what Scripture says: "Now I am making the whole of creation new" (Rev. 21:5).

Not that I love death because it dissolves my last remaining strength.

I love death because it "makes all things new."

Whenever I see a slobbering, trembling old man, I make an effort to think of him in the body of a happy baby. Whenever I look at a woman tragically enduring the ugliness and inroads of old age, the fruit of time, I put my imagination to work and think of her as a teenage girl racing through fields of flowers to meet her sweetheart.

I love death because it gives me back life.

I love death because I believe in the resurrection.

Now, that is something I can get excited about!

What would have been the point of all my efforts to believe, of all my hoping against hope if, when I got to that moment, I were to settle for nothingness? Or worse, immobility, an eternal paralysis?

No, I do not settle for that, and I tell you, or rather, I shout at you:

"I believe in the life everlasting!"

I believe in my everlasting body as an immortal babe.

I believe in my running like a little boy to meet my God, as when long ago, after school, I ran like crazy to meet my father, who had come to take me for a walk in the fields along the Po.

But even more I believe in death, because I shall finally see the kingdom, which here below I have only descried through the mist, and dreamed about. I shall see the Church in its final transparency.

I shall see my mother again.

I shall see my friends again.

I shall see righteousness.

I shall see the banquet.

I shall see people at peace at last and able to love one another.

I shall see Christ!

There, I know, I shall be thunderstruck at his beauty and shall never have to leave him again.

Also because, as the "Lamb that was slain," he has become "worthy to open the scroll and break the seals" (see Rev. 5:9).

And he will open them.

And we shall read all the mysteries. We shall know the whys and wherefores of history, of the succession of the generations, of all the tears and bloodshed.

Who turns the pages of the Book will be Mary of Nazareth, the only creature worthy to help her son in explaining these things to us. Mark well, I am not dreaming; I am reading my faith, my hope. This is why I tell you that death is one of God's great inventions. What would we be without death?

Who feels like living on in a nursing home where people have put you with all their love and pills?

Not I.

And I invoke death as a transit.

This will be my Passover.

This will be the gate of heaven. This will be the resurrection.

And here I must tell you another secret I have discovered recently: I am sure, when death's hammer smashes me like an olive; in that instant I shall see all the whys of life: in that instant I shall say, "Now I understand why death is this great fact throughout the cosmos. In death was hidden the very secret of life."

And a great "Oh!" of wonder will rise from my being.

Quake not, then, my soul, and have no fear.

Look straight ahead and smile one last time.

As the Spirit glided over chaos in the beginning and God created the universe, now he will return, to hover once more and make all things new again.

Precisely because I believe in God, I know what death is, and it cannot frighten me.

Or at least it will only frighten me mentally — and with good reason, for I shall feel such a powerful wrench and an even more obvious difference.

Come then, O death, my death!

I shall welcome you as my sweetheart, I shall embrace you as my sister.

I shall greet you as mother.

I do not ask you not to be painful; the memory of my brother Jesus' death will remind me to keep quiet and acquiesce.

I shall ask you to have mercy on my weakness.

I shall ask you to make me one with all my fellow beings dying in pain.

I shall ask you to help me forget all about my sins and be brave enough to believe in God's mercy.

I shall ask you to act quickly. Yes, this I shall ask of you. But more than anything else, I shall ask you to give me your love right away.

Here below, forsaking all the rest, I have been left with three things, and I have sought to live them: "faith, hope, and love" (1 Cor. 13:13).

As to faith, I have succeeded, a tiny crumb of a bit. I have always been fond of faith as of a great risk to run, and I have loved to stake it all like a master-card in my hand.

As to hope, I have done better. My mother transmitted to me in my blood her unbeatable optimism, her urge to sing and live.

But as to charity, to love, what are we to say?

This is where my weak point has been.

Here I have not succeeded very well. On the contrary, I have barely understood what the rapture of service and total self-giving can be.

Paul's mighty statement " ... if I have faith in all its fullness, to move mountains, but without love, then I am nothing at all" (1 Cor. 13:2) has always tormented me and made me weep, too.

In my boundless inability to love, God has revealed to me what God's folly is.

Yes, through the darkness of my selfishness, he has shown me the blinding lights of his love.

What a clash, between the poverty of human love and the madness of God!

How I have suffered in the darkness of my rational way of judging things!

And how clear within me was the vision of the "emergency exit" that would have saved me: the madness of love!

But I was unable to open it, being held back by the fear of losing all.

I actually had the idea that, were I to give myself ... I would lose everything!

On the contrary, I should have gained everything!

As you did, Jesus, on Calvary.

Nor have I been able to ask, with St. Francis:

Lord Jesus, two graces I ask of you before I die.

First, in my soul and in my body, to feel as far as possible, the sorrow which you, sweet Jesus, endured in the hour of your most bitter passion.

Second, in my heart, as far as possible, to feel that extraordinary love with which you, O Son of God, were inflamed, to the point of being willing to undergo so great a passion for us sinners.

No, my God, I have not been able.

And this is why I want to die.

So that I can go instantly mad under the hammer blows of your Spirit. So I can vault the barricade of my own insuperable limitations. What I have been incapable of doing here, I count on doing at my Passover, when you will at last come into my being and burn it away as in the fire.

What joy, Lord, this, your loving-madness! When I think that you will transmit this madness to me too, I descry the reality of the kingdom, as a transit from the human to the divine, for which you are preparing us — and as the joy of living forever with you.

What more shall I say to you in my leave-taking, old friends?

I do not know. Shall I say that you will go through hard times? No need to tell you that; everyone knows it.

The very stones cry out....

Do not go into life without dreaming of building yourselves a house to live in, a vocation to find fulfillment in, and children to play with.

I know that you have temptations against faith. How could it be otherwise, in a world where humanity by force of intellect, has succeeded in walking on the moon and in transforming the earth into a single insufferable gangster-land by its sick heart?

When you are tempted, do not retreat a single step. God will help you.

And perhaps the better to help you, he will give you a little poverty but the real kind, not the romantic kind flaunted by European Christians of my time.

He may even be forced to lead you back to the Egypt of ancient slavery, or even to the dreadful loneliness of Babylon.

Whatever happens to you, do not retreat a single step.

This too will pass, and God abides forever.

For me, all this is over and I have the feeling of having attained the goal.

But if I have won, it's because God has won, and if you too win it will be because God wins in you.

Together let us recall Jesus' words when he bade farewell to his own: "Do not let your hearts be troubled. Trust in God..." (1 John 4:1).

Ah, look ... we could finish by reading one of the last pages of the Book of Revelation together:

I saw a new heaven and a new earth; the first heaven and the first earth had disappeared now, and there was no longer any sea.

I saw the holy city, and the new Jerusalem, coming down from God out of heaven, as beautiful as a bride all dressed for her husband.

Then I heard a loud voice call from the throne, "Here God lives among men. He will make his home among them; they shall be his people, and he will be their God; his name is God-with-them. He will wipe away all tears from their eyes; there will be no more death, and no more mourning or sadness. The world of the past has gone." (Rev. 21:1–4)

And the answer is contained in the splendid finale:

"Yes, I am coming soon!" Amen!
 "Come, Lord Jesus!"
 "May the grace of the Lord Jesus be with you all. Amen!" (see Rev. 22:20–21).

                                        — *I Sought and I Found*

Bibliography

The following books by Carlo Carretto have been translated and published in English. They are listed in order of their original Italian publication.

Made in Heaven. Trans. Alan Neame (original: *Famiglia, piccola chiesa,* 1949). London: Darton, Longman and Todd, 1978.

Letters from the Desert. Trans. Rose Mary Hancock (original: *Lettere dal deserto,* 1964). Maryknoll, N.Y.: Orbis Books and London: Darton, Longman and Todd, 1972.

Love Is for Living. Trans. Jeremy Moiser (original: *Ciago che conta é amare,* 1966). London: Darton, Longman and Todd and Maryknoll, N.Y.: Orbis Books, 1976.

In Search of the Beyond. Trans. Sarah Fawcett (original: *Al di la delle Cose,* 1969). London: Darton, Longman and Todd and Maryknoll: N.Y.: Orbis Books, 1975.

The God Who Comes. Trans. Rose Mary Hancock (original: *Il Dio che vigne,* 1971). Maryknoll, N.Y.: Orbis Books, 1974.

Summoned by Love. Trans. Alan Neame (original: *Padre Mio, Mi Abbandono a Te,* 1975). London: Darton, Longman and Todd, 1977. Maryknoll, N.Y.: Orbis Books, 1978.

The Desert in the City. Trans. Barbara Wall (original: *Il Deserto Nella Città,* 1978). London: Collins, 1979.

Blessed Are You Who Believed. Trans. Barbara Wall (original: *Beata te che hai creduto,* 1980). Tunbridge Wells: Burns & Oates, 1982. Maryknoll, N.Y.: Orbis Books, 1983.

I, Francis. Trans. Robert R. Barr (original: *Io Francesco,* 1980). Maryknoll, N.Y.: Orbis Books, 1982.

I Sought and I Found: My Experience of God and the Church.
Trans. Robert R. Barr (original: *Ho cercato e ho trovato,*
1983). Maryknoll, N.Y.: Orbis Books, 1984.

Why O Lord? The Inner Meaning of Suffering. Trans. Robert R.
Barr (original: *Perche Signore? Il Dolore: Segreto Nascoto
nei Secoli,* 1985). Maryknoll, N.Y.: Orbis Books, 1986.

Journey without End. Trans. Alan Neame (original: *Un Camino
Senza Fine,* 1986). Notre Dame: Ave Maria Press, 1989.

And God Saw That It Was Good. Trans. Alan Neame (original: *E Dio vide che era cosa buona,* 1988). Slough: St. Paul
Publications, 1989. Maryknoll, N.Y.: Orbis Books, 1990.

Letters to Dolcidia: 1954–1983. Ed. Gian Carlo Sibilia, trans.
Michael J. Smith (original: *Lettere a Dolcidia,* 1989). London: HarperCollins and Maryknoll, N.Y.: Orbis Books,
1991.

The Desert Journal: A Diary 1954–55. Trans. Alison Swaisland
Bucci (original: *El-Abiodh: diario spirituale 1954–1955,*
1990). London: HarperCollins and Maryknoll, N.Y.: Orbis
Books, 1992.

Acknowledgments

Orbis Books is grateful to the following publishers for permission to reprint material:

Cittá Nuova Editrice, Rome, for material from *The God Who Comes.*

Cittadella Editrice, Assisi, for material from: *I Sought and I Found,* second edition revised and enlarged, copyright © 1983 by Cittadella Editrice; *I, Francis* copyright © 1980 by Cittadella Editrice; and *In Search of the Beyond,* English translation copyright © 1975 by Darton, Longman and Todd Ltd., London.

St. Paul Publications, Slough, England, for material from *And God Saw That It Was Good,* English translation copyright © 1989 by St. Paul Publications, Slough, England.

Burns & Oates/Search Press for material from *Blessed Are You Who Believed,* English translation copyright © 1982 by Search Press, Kent.

La Scuola Editrice, Brescia, for material from *Letters from the Desert,* English translation copyright © 1972 by Orbis Books.

Edizioni Morcelliana, Brescia, for material from *Why O Lord?* English translation copyright © 1986 by Orbis Books.

Darton, Longman and Todd Ltd., London, for material from: *Love Is for Living,* English translation copyright © 1976 by